MISSY HAMILNOOK REFLECTS

on early childhood education

ALICITA HAMILTON

with photographs by WARREN HAMILTON

Printed in the United States of America by Lightning Source, Inc.

ISBN 978-0-9837470-5-5

Library of Congress Control Number 2013948142

Published 2013 by BookCrafters, Parker, Colorado.
SAN-859-6352, BookCrafters@comcast.net

Copies of this book may be ordered from www.bookcrafters.net
and other online bookstores.

DEDICATED TO THE MEMORY OF

MOLLY MASON JONES

Professor of Psychology, Scripps College, Claremont, California
Director of Mary B. Eyre Nursery School, 1939-1967

She believed this story should be told

Acknowledgments

I am deeply grateful to

Kirsten Morgan, a gifted writer, who found a way to break my thirty-year-cycle of procrastination and provided frequent encouragement and support during the year it took to write this story.

Heather Thomas, who helped me with many ideas about the content of this memoir as well as publishing options, and who met with me regularly (as did Kirsten) to comment on what I had written.

Carol Ehrlich, who recruited me to work at DU and provided enthusiastic support as well as careful editing of this manuscript.

Dorothy Howe Koenig Hoien, my mother, who saved my letters to her from 1950 to 1986, arranged chronologically, and returned them to me in 1986 shortly before her death in 1987. She urged me to write a book about my teaching experiences.

My children, **Jim**, **Kathy**, and **Larry**, who adjusted seamlessly to life with a working mother and willingly shared their gerbils, ducks, and tortoise with my preschool children.

Alicita Hamilton

Table of Contents

Introduction

"Life can only be understood backwards; but it must be lived forward."
Søren Kierkegaard

The first hint of fall color was in the silver maples on a sunny Monday morning when I swung onto the freeway to drive across town to a new job. I had been hired two weeks earlier by the Speech and Hearing Clinic of the University of Denver to be the preschool teacher for six children who were hearing impaired. This was to be a temporary position funded by a research grant, but it evolved into a twenty-year commitment to develop and implement preschool programs for language-impaired youngsters.

From 1962 through 1982, I worked with children who had various problems related to speech and language. For the first two years, my preschool population was limited to hearing impaired children enrolled for study as part of the research grant. When that study ended, I was invited to remain on the staff. We gradually changed the preschool population to include children with other types of communication disorders, and after 1974 we added children with normal language development, adapting to then-new "mainstreaming" concepts. The photographs in this book show youngsters from all of these groups.

Language development in young children can reflect a spectrum of problems. Referrals were made by pediatricians, medical centers, welfare agencies, and preschool programs. Some children joined us because their mothers were concerned about the clarity of their children's speech. A few of the children stuttered, a few were multiply handicapped, and many showed significant delay in language development. We worked with children who were neurologically impaired or showed behavior considered to be autistic. Some lived in conditions that minimized opportunities for growth.

My interest in early childhood came from my efforts to understand, as a student of psychology, the dynamics of my own childhood, and from the model my mother provided as an educator of elementary school children. She was, sequentially, teacher, supervisor, and coordinator of elementary education in the Los Angeles County School system, and was California State President of the prestigious honorary group of women educators, Delta Kappa Gamma International. She co-authored a curriculum guide, *Their First Years in School*, and taught many summer workshops on California university campuses.

1

In the 1930s and 1940s the curriculum of the elementary schools in Los Angeles County reflected the new progressive education movement, with leadership from the University of Chicago. I was a beneficiary of that philosophical heritage. As the only child of a single working mother, I often joined her at teacher training workshops in interesting places. My becoming the preschool teacher in a challenging setting was a natural step forward in my own life. As I reflect, it almost seems predetermined!

From the time I left California with my geologist husband to move to Oklahoma, to Tennessee, and then to settle in Colorado, I wrote many letters to my mother revealing my feelings about what was happening, which she saved, filed by year, and gave to me in the mid- 1980s. I include excerpts from them here, in *italics*. She hoped I would write about my experiences, and the letters proved to be an invaluable resource for *Missy Hamilnook Reflects*. She never responded directly to my comments, but always helped when I asked for curriculum suggestions and for picture books, song books, and music for rhythmic activities.

For the first fifteen years, our university preschool provided planned indoor and outdoor activities for our preschool children, in addition to a daily half hour of individual speech therapy. We were a center for early childhood education, and also provided diagnostic and therapeutic services. In the 1970s, we opened the morning class to a majority of children whose language development was on track, "mainstreaming" in that group a few children with communication problems. We hoped to provide models for the at-risk children and to provide opportunities for our college students to observe normal language development. The plan was a boon for all participants.

The most important theme emerging as I write is my belief in the importance of play in providing experiential learning. **Play is the work of the young child**. Play with other children, in carefully planned experiences, immerses children in the learning process. Play enables opportunities for discovery, and consolidates experiences in dramatic interactions. It lays the groundwork for comprehension, which builds a foundation for symbolic and abstract thought. Descriptions of play centers, curriculum materials, and relationships in this account indicate ways I implemented this process. My reflections cover what I did, and why, over twenty years.

A secondary theme is the changing national atmosphere of the turbulent 1960s and 1970s, which intruded on the protected bubble of my professional and family life. The assassination of President Kennedy, and the enactment of the Civil Rights Act of 1964, led to enormous sudden change. We discovered the child living in poverty. Colorado educators mobilized to train teachers, to establish Head Start centers, and to join forces with the National Association for the Education of Young Children (NAEYC) as professional educators in the Colorado Association (CAEYC). Our mission as early childhood educators was suddenly greatly enlarged.

The publication in 1960 of Betty Friedan's book *The Feminine Mystique* led to the beginning of the women's movement for equity at work and raised issues about the status of women at the university. The Vietnam War and the shooting of the students at Kent State University resonated to affect students and campuses across the country. It was a time of turmoil, and of transition for me as my children came of age on college campuses in opposite corners of the country.

Early childhood education is again in transition. Are we teaching academics soon enough? Do we need to provide preschool for every child, and if so, how? Our education system is being evaluated in terms of global competition. Universal preschool education has been suggested to mitigate our national social inequities. We need to pause and reflect on what plans are in process for our youngest citizens. The structure and stability of our families are at risk, and more social change looms on our horizon.

In the following accounts, all children's names have been changed, but all descriptions are of actual children, fictitiously named. All adults at the University of Denver are given their real names. Names of preschool adults in Chapter One have been changed, except for my longtime friend Connie.

Chapter One
A Telephone Call

The students were assembling in the classroom as the afternoon sun streamed through large windows. I had just hurried in with my assembled lecture notes from the preschool where I had spent the day supervising morning and afternoon classes of small children. Suddenly through the open classroom door ran exuberant, tow-headed four-year-old Christopher on his way home from preschool. Close behind, his mother tried to steer him toward the main door of the building. On seeing me in this new habitat, he shouted, to the delight of the students, "Nere's Missy Hamilnook!" My new name stuck for the remainder of my twenty years at the University of Denver.

In the beginning

The story began when my telephone rang mid-morning on a hot July day in 1962. It was Carol, who was working on her Ph.D. in audiology at the University of Denver Speech and Hearing Clinic. "We're looking for a preschool teacher. A half-day temporary job, part of research which will be finished in two years. Would you be interested? You'd be working five mornings a week with a group of hearing-impaired young children."

"But I don't know anything about deaf children," I said, startled.

"You don't have to. In fact that's an advantage for this particular grant. With your background you'd be ideal. Want to come for an interview with Joe, our director?" I would, and I did.

Carol and I had become friends working together at the Unitarian Church Sunday School Program—she as director, I as preschool teacher. She was aware of my training at Scripps College, my experience in California public schools as a kindergarten teacher, and, most recently, my two years in a private preschool in Lakewood. She knew that in that program I had been working with special children referred from the University of Colorado Medical Center.

The interview with Joe went well. I liked him and felt he was someone I would be comfortable with as director. That proved to be true. When I met him, I once more disclaimed any expertise with a clear statement, "I don't know anything about deaf children!" Joe told me that was fine. He wanted someone who could provide the children with the best early childhood program possible–a program that would be considered enriching for children with normal hearing.

Joe's research was directed toward assessing the effectiveness of a new concept, an "Acoupedic Program," to help hearing impaired young children develop speech and language. The plan was to fit them as young as possible with hearing aids, offer regular speech therapy and a normal preschool experience, surround them with opportunities for language stimulation, and avoid dependence on lip-reading. Children were encouraged to "listen," and their teacher encouraged to provide lots of narration. It was a controversial project in the community of teachers of the deaf, who mostly preferred sign language or lip-reading.

Joe said he specifically did not want a trained "teacher of the deaf," who might display hearing charts of individual children on the walls of a classroom as reminders of the extent of a hearing deficit. The children he was studying were fitted with hearing aids with the expectation that as they began to hear and listen to speech, they would begin to use words. He wanted me to talk to them as though they could hear everything I said. That directive was a good fit for me and became the foundation of a philosophy for working with "special" children that emphasized what a child could do, rather than what he could not do. I was pleased to learn in my early weeks that Joe expressed delight in my work to others. After he left, new faculty who joined our staff were equally supportive and enthusiastic.

Joe discussed my part-time salary. I told him that I had been earning $100 a month in Lakewood for a nine month school year. My honesty and the resulting salary I agreed to with him would become an endless see-saw in future years. Joe said, "We can do better than that," and offered me $2,400 for the three Quarter academic year—fall, winter, and spring—with almost a month free in December. I accepted with delight. A new door had opened to me, and I wanted to walk through it.

Why was I eager to walk through that door?

My preceding two years as teacher in a private Lakewood preschool included generic experiences and challenges. Our school had an enrollment of about sixty children and a staff of seven women. Three of us had unusual backgrounds. Anne was a nurse, who moved on several years later to join the faculty of the School of Nursing in the University of Colorado Medical Center. Connie, who had degrees in journalism and psychology, taught one of our preschool classes. She later became a counseling psychologist at the Denver Florence Crittenden Home for Expectant Mothers, and years later became Director of the Day Care Center at the University of California in Santa Barbara. My degree was in child psychology and early childhood education.

Each of the staff was paid $100 a month to work from 8:30 to 12:00 five mornings a week. Our small charges were three to five years old, divided by age into classes of ten. Then as now, the auto mechanics who care for our cars earn more per hour than do preschool teachers. Our rented space was the Sunday School area in a large church, and on Fridays we put toys away on shelves in hinged locked bookcases which had wheels for easy moving. Some of our outdoor equipment was shared with the Church. We were expected to sanitize tables, chairs, and bathrooms, prepare and clean up art projects, sweep the floors, and move equipment as needed. Fifty years later, hygienic matters and housekeeping continue to be chores for preschool teachers.

A letter to my mother in 1960 reads: *I feel more like a furniture mover and scrub woman than an educator. Friday, in a howling blizzard, we moved one slide, one set of parallel bars, two space trainers, and three enormous rubber tires indoors from the playground. On Monday, three of our staff called in reporting flu. I don't know how long I can maintain my idealistic ardor. It is darn hard work. I feel a little weak myself.*

Connie would lean on her broom when we swept floors, and bemoan that our chores should not include "janitorial services." Our Director, Marian, versed in psychiatric matters, responded to our complaints with the Freudian twist that we were simply voicing a basic feminine conflict. "Nonsense," countered Connie, who disliked sanitizing tables and bathrooms and sweeping floors as much as I did. We had cleaning women at home— why should we go to work to do such? Marian herself relied on her mother and her teachers to manage daily affairs at the school! All of this was current practice about the time Betty Friedan published her book *The Feminine Mystique*. Many of us who read her book began to question our goals and our lives.

It was not possible to set up learning centers within our small Sunday School classrooms. In the 1960s, many private preschools in Denver were housed in churches with similar limitations. We had three-shelf bookcases on wheels to hold toys and materials in each room. They had hinged doors with padlocks, and we pushed them into corners to avoid interference with needs of Sunday School. Preschool activities centered on the contents of these shelves. One case had cardboard building blocks, and cars, trucks, and dolls for dramatic play. The room with the piano was our music center, with rhythm instruments, phonograph, and records (I was one of two staff members who could play the piano). A third room had scissors, paste, paints, play-dough, and other manipulative materials.

The preschool morning for the children was from 9:00 to 11:30, and always included outdoor play. Staff members brought us a snack indoors before we went outside—basically milk and graham crackers with occasional other treats to celebrate birthdays or holidays. We sang our way through the morning with "this is the way we put away toys" (to the tune of Mulberry Bush) as we periodically moved to another room to change activities. Singing was intended to soften teacher announcements of "clean-up time."

We teachers were mostly anonymous to the parents we served. Our director chose to identify the staff to parents and children by our first names. Marian's mother, our parent greeter at the door, was Miss Betty. I was Miss Alice, an appropriate simplification of my first name, which had once been pronounced by the two-year-old next door to me as "La-la-tho-tho." We were not encouraged to counsel with parents. Marian enjoyed interviewing parents and selecting children for the preschool, and preferred to do all parent counseling herself. However, she gave me several wonderful opportunities to work with professionals from the CU Medical Center, which laid the foundation for my later work at the University of Denver.

Marian liked to invite psychiatric nurse interns to observe "her" teachers with their classes. She warned me that the nurses were "very bright and very perceptive." The nurses were at pains to assure me that they were not there to "evaluate" me, and I told them that I welcomed their observation. They seemed surprised at my response to what I perceived as patronizing comments. One asked me if I had ever heard of something called an Oedipus Complex. I explained that I had majored in psychology at Scripps College and had since taken several graduate courses in psychology.

It is all too common for early childhood educators to be regarded as lightly educated sub-professionals. Funding for preschool education and training for teachers is characteristically low on the scale of academic priorities. Despite this assumption, James Heckman, professor of economics at the University of Chicago, wrote that "enriched early intervention programs . . . have had their biggest effect on non-cognitive skills: motivation, self-control and time preference," skills that are related to the essential "executive function . . . the very definition of ourselves as people." (Executive function refers to ordering thoughts and processing information, maximizing memory, minimizing distractions, learning to remain focused.) He further commented that "acquisition of these skills has been shown to predict academic achievement more reliably than IQ tests . . . the most economically efficient way to remediate for disadvantage . . . is to invest in children when they are young."

Marian assigned a nurse working on her graduate degree in psychiatric nursing to observe in one of my classes. Her task was to do an observational study of a "normal" child selected by me. I found the nurse unprepared for a "normal" group of preschool children. About her I wrote to my mother: *I was able to select a "normal" child, Heidi, in my group of ten for her to study. One little boy stutters, one has epilepsy, one has a severe hearing loss. My observer began a conversation with me as the class was in session about how the schizophrenic child views the world. The discussion was quickly aborted when children began flying paper airplanes around the room. I didn't even try to mix easel paints that morning but did solicit her help to scrape mud off shoes following outdoor play. By the end of the morning, I was beyond caring if she was critical of my musical talents when I sang folk tunes as I played my autoharp for resting children.*

Heidi

Heidi was blonde, blue-eyed, round and solid, a serene and self-confident three year old. She had just discovered that if she coughed loudly several times adults would offer her a glass of water. Some time later, with that behavior outgrown, she began to look for a non-existent cut on her finger, and asked Miss Betty for a band aid. (Our band aids were decorated with cartoon characters.) Betty was always willing, in her anxious way, to do this kind of thing. After a few repeats, Heidi forgot about band aids and went on to other things. When Heidi asked Miss Betty for band aids, she was learning and practicing a valuable skill. As Harvard psychologist Burton White wrote in *The First Three Years of Life,* it is critical for a child to learn to use an adult as a resource.

In my letter to my mother I wrote that the nurse observer commented to me with concern that "we wouldn't want Heidi to learn to separate herself from her peers with hypochondriasis now, would we?" I responded with appropriate gravity but was bemused by the psychiatric intensity with which occasional beginning students over-react to the passing behavior of small children.

Stephanie

Then there was Stephanie, who wandered around in a dazed, determined, and isolated little cloud. The only way she knew what might be worth doing was to see someone else doing it. Storytime became a challenge–she found she could talk as loudly and continuously as I could. The boys discovered she was good material for sport, and they could elicit a piercing yell by kidnapping her doll. She was neither angry nor aggressive. She just lived in her own foggy little world. We transferred her to the "least mature" group in our school.

Mark

I received a valentine from Mark, who has moved far away. I hoped he would find a new teacher who would really love him and help him handle his impulsive behavior which made a misery of our Monday, Wednesday, Friday class. His mother and father each came separately to thank me for the changes wrought in Mark. His father said Mark refused to move unless he could take Miss Alice with him. Such is the stuff that makes teaching rewarding.

Christmas gifts and notes of appreciation are common and treasured, but most of us who teach young children disappear from their early vestigial memories.

My two years at the Lakewood preschool set the stage for my career as an early childhood educator. I had been at home raising my own three children for more than a decade, and my youngest child, Jim, would start kindergarten in the fall of 1960. I knew that I would miss him, and was determined to release my children to become independent as they grew older and to build a life for myself outside our home. A favorite quotation of mine reads: "There are only two gifts we can give our children, one is roots, the other is wings." A half-day job would allow me to support them in their school activities as well as to provide a gentle transition to work outside my home.

In front of the looking glass

I was anonymous "Miss Alice" during my Lakewood preschool days. At the University, I became a professional woman with a full name.

I will never forget my first day with six small hearing impaired children wearing hearing aids. A week earlier I had gone to the Clinic to assess the available equipment, to tidy and set up the room in the aging temporary WWII wooden building. I took in large pictures of characters in nursery rhymes framed with tag-board to hang at children's eye level, where their own art work would be displayed in time. I arranged "centers" for learning: a housekeeping center with kitchen sink, cupboards and stove; an art center with easel and paints; a table with puzzles and manipulative materials. I selected books for a quiet reading nook and instruments for an active music center around the old upright piano. I intended to be the facilitating adult as children interacted with materials, each other, and with me. Experiential learning for children with teacher as designer and helper was to be my goal for twenty years.

I was probably more eager and anxious than the children on that first morning. For a few of the children, I replaced the teacher from the year before. For others, I was their first teacher. I was keenly aware that I was not a "teacher of the deaf," which created anxiety for some mothers of returning children.

I was just starting the morning with my six hearing impaired children, all brand new to me, when in came Alice, our supervisor of therapy, leading two-year-old Vicki. Vicki had cataracts in both eyes, very little if any hearing, no hearing aids as yet, and that morning had broken her glasses before her mother brought her to school. Alice said she wanted to "try her out to see how she'd get along." With one look at my stunned face, Alice, holding Vicki's tiny hand, turned away to leave quietly. Five minutes later Alice returned to say that they'd bring her later in the week and have our psychologist, Esther, observe through the one way mirror and evaluate her. Thursday they brought her back. She stayed with us for about an hour, after which observation everyone agreed nursery school wasn't the solution for little Vicki. At least her glasses were fixed by Thursday.

A large one-way mirror in one corner of the room allowed anyone interested to watch the preschool activities. A pull-down shade to cover the window was on my side, but I seldom used it. The booth was used (often without notifying me) by parents, faculty, staff, students, and visitors. One-way mirrors constitute a magnet to people. I was pleased to be a demonstration teacher, but sometimes felt that I lived in a goldfish bowl.

Learning centers as curriculum

The large preschool room offered the opportunity to develop multiple learning centers, which had not been possible in the Lakewood preschool. Learning centers provide the framework for curriculum, and highlight the fact that play is the work of young children. As they experiment with paint, sand, and water, children are making new discoveries, and reinforcing early scientific curiosity. In using a variety of art materials, they are engaging creative skills to make a product. By entering pretend play with others, they are laying the foundation for developing symbolic thought.

With grant money, Joe provided me with whatever props I requested for the learning centers. There were many good pieces of equipment to begin with. I placed the housekeeping center in the corner of the room with the sink and cupboard facing the one-way mirror. Sometimes the sink would be filled with soapy water for washing dishes, pots, and pans. Other mornings it could be bath water for a baby doll. The children loved to watch themselves in the mirror as they played house.

Mirrors enhance development of self-concept. Some children become obsessive performers in front of a mirror but that was not true for children in this group. I sought creative props that could enhance dramatic play and suggest re-enactment of experiences and roles. Furniture for the play house area included sink, cupboard, stove, cooking utensils, dishes, an ironing board with iron, a broom, dolls with bed and clothing, and buggy. Clothes for "dressing up" were available—shoes, hats, dresses, coats, bridal veils, tutus, and such in a small closet with hangers. With appropriate props a center could be converted to offer multiple dramatic play opportunities

In 1963, the John Tracy Clinic Demonstration Nursery School for children with impaired hearing in Los Angeles had a large staff and an organized group of helping parents. With many hands there can be play centers suggesting emergency road repair (tricycles outdoors), orthopedic medicine (dolls with broken arms), protective services (fire-fighting and traffic control on the playground), construction engineers (block building), and heavy equipment operations (small dump trucks). They believed in 1963, as I still do now, that "play is the 'soul' of the nursery school curriculum." Preparation for a variety of play opportunities is labor intensive, and a teacher working alone is more limited. The cooperative preschool where parents participate as helpers in setting up activities, putting away materials and props, and cleaning up makes it much easier for a teacher to provide a variety of imaginative play themes.

Chapter Two
Inside the One-way Mirror

Artists, architects, musicians, mommies and doctors at work

The first challenge—saying goodbye to Mom

The first day at school is the first hurdle. How does the child say goodbye to Mom at the preschool door? Preschool is an extension upward of the home and the extension downward of the school, our two primary socializing institutions. It is the time in the young child's life when issues of trust and autonomy (separateness from parents) are of concern. Much has been written about "separation anxiety," which, unresolved, can create troubled lives. Preschool teachers recognize the need to ease this transition for both parents and children.

Most of our hearing impaired children were remarkably ready to start preschool. Learning centers in our classroom invited them to explore and play. Most who were initially shy quickly found things they wanted to do.

When a child appeared anxious we would invite a mother to come for the morning, bring a book to read and sit in a distant corner of the room, hopefully absorbed in her book. Several years later we began to start the year with "graduated entrance" at which two or three couples, mother and child, were invited to spend the morning in our preschool together getting acquainted over milk and cookies. The child could engage in a sample routine morning.

Debbie and Jack

Debbie and Jack had not yet celebrated their third birthdays by the first day of school, and were the two youngest children in the Acoupedic group. Both of them separated comfortably from their mothers. My first impression was that they could have been two happy little people in any preschool group. Typical of their age, they engaged either in solitary play, or in parallel play alongside another child. Debbie was well coordinated and interested in seeking new activities. Jack often wore a happy grin as he finger painted, or more seriously considered his block construction of a garage for a truck.

Two-year-olds love to fill and empty things—wagons, buckets, cups. Or stack small blocks and knock them down. Ping pong balls fascinate them with their capacity to bounce noisily and move unpredictably on hard surfaces. Stuffed animals can become special as "lovies" that fill a developmental need.

Three-year-olds love to mimic family activities or an aggressive TV character such as Batman. They are collectors and gatherers. The real and the pretend are not separated in their dramatic play. The child becomes what he represents.

Max

Max, three years old, separated from his mother without incident. Initially shy, he headed for the kitchen sink to wash dishes as soon as he arrived at school. After his first morning, I made sure soapsuds were available. Wearing an apron (a small man's shirt worn in reverse) he scrubbed dishes, pots and pans, dried them on a towel, and watched himself thoughtfully in the mirror. He was a slender child with large handsome dark brown eyes and a manner of pleased concentration at whatever he did. He developed a wide variety of interests, loving to paint at the easel, finger paint, build with unit blocks, whack the big drum, and sit with the group watching and listening to flannel board stories. By his second year he was asking for the paint colors he wanted to use. After two years with us he went on to the special education program in Denver Public Schools, and in his teens celebrated his Bar Mitzvah!

Music

From their first day the children responded enthusiastically to rhythmic activities for which I played the piano. We had an aging upright piano, a record player, and an excellent set of rhythm instruments. From earliest days, I used the piano to highlight transitions from one activity to another. I would play several arpeggios or a short melody to indicate that it was time to put away toys and gather as a group at the piano. Sometimes I brought my autoharp from home or played short records, or sang simple folk songs. The children were not yet ready to use words in song, but greatly enjoyed rhythmic activity, bouncing and leaping around. I had a repertoire of piano music for slithering like snakes, or jumping, hopping like toads, bouncing like balls, flying like airplanes, spinning like tops, or popping like popcorn in a hot pan.

Through creative movement set to music children developed coordination, a sense of rhythm, self-confidence in what their bodies could do, self-expression, and often released pent-up energy. I collected simple, clear pictures suggesting movement activities and hung them on a large key ring to be easily flipped for ideas. I brought in both puppets-on-strings and hand puppets to dance to music or to visually enhance a story. Four-year-old Mary Ann, who had been in the Acoupedic Program the previous year, was my helpful cohort in our music activities. She taught me the importance of having a model within a preschool group. Children learn from each other.

Mary Ann

Mary Ann was an attractive little girl with bright brown eyes and brown hair carefully groomed to just cover her hearing aids. She loved to come to school, to play the drums and the piano. She experimented with sounds on the keyboard and would try high and low notes at the same time. She engaged in dramatic play in our playhouse corner, playing cooperatively with children in the group who were ready to do that. During her time with us she began to use words clearly enough to be understood. I was pleased many years later to hear from her mother. The family had moved to New York, and Mary Ann was in high school wanting to play on the basketball team. She needed permission to play a contact sport while wearing a hearing aid. Her mother called to ask me for a letter of support. I was delighted to write one and sought other letters for her as well.

Art

Creative opportunities to work with paint, clay, scissors, colored paper and paste at each child's own level of competence were available. Easel paints were mixed and placed in trays on each side of the easel so that two children could paint at the same time. Finger painting, cutting and pasting collages, and working with clay were available alternately with puzzles and tasks requiring fine motor skills. Art activities were primarily self-chosen and self-directed, but prepared ahead of class. Adult initiated crafts were minimized except to create a few holiday gifts for parents, which the parents treasured. My favorite December craft was a hand-print in clay, fired for permanence and wrapped in paper decorated with finger paint.

When the question is asked "What does the preschool teach regarding art?" the answer should be that all of the elements that may be perceived through the senses are included: texture, shape, color, line, and value (light and dark). While adults are responsible for preparing art activities and mopping-up afterward, we tried to maximize freedom for the children to be creative, and we phrased any necessary directions positively by telling children **what to do** rather than **what not to do.** For example, when finger paint was smeared on a cheek, the suggestion was made firmly, as hands were placed back on

14

the paper that, "the paint stays on the paper." With the four-year-olds, who could be depended upon to distinguish the edible from the inedible, we sometimes finger painted with chocolate pudding, and then, licking fingers was ok.

Adults were also cautioned against asking "What is that?" with regard to any painting or product. If compelled to say anything, they were advised to say something in the nature of "Tell me about it." The important thing was to value whatever the child could do by framing, displaying, and acknowledging her work. An affirmation of the child's product can provide a reflection of self.

Some days the table which held self-directed art activities served instead as a place to work puzzles or to use a variety of manipulative materials encouraging fine motor coordination or perceptual skills. Sometimes we had simple cooking projects. In the late 1970s, we added sewing projects and bought a water table to hold either water or sand. Water tables are about three feet wide and six feet long and the right height for children to stand or sit at play. They have removable plastic tubs that can be emptied of sand or water.

Equipment—what we had, what we didn't have

The preschool had some wonderful equipment before I arrived. There were large hollow hardwood blocks for building rooms and walls—each block 12" by 12" by 4". There were large wooden cars and trucks, a hardwood rocking boat that held six children, an indoor jungle gym, and a large set of multi-shaped small solid hardwood unit blocks for building roads, bridges, towers, rooms, garages, or whatever else children wanted to create. The small hardwood unit blocks are among the most valuable tools we can provide young children in a preschool or kindergarten classroom. Children make discoveries with blocks about size, shape, symmetry, mapping a construction, measurements, depth, width, height, and length, all forerunners of mathematical comprehension of size, shape and number.

Sets of hardwood unit blocks were first developed in the early 1900s and are good for home use. They also make an ideal activity in a preschool classroom for interactive play and experiential learning. A November 13, 2013 article in the New York Times stated that these blocks are "helpful to build 21st century skills essential to success in corporate America. Such skills can provide an antidote to fine motor-skills deficits and difficulty with unstructured activity, problems (of) too much time in front of screens (and) overly academic preschools."

In our classroom, putting toys away after use also served as a perceptual training tool. Blocks went on shelves marked with pictured cut-outs of the different shapes. My family has had a home set that belonged to my husband as a child and, in time, became the toys of our two youngest grandchildren. Some of the pieces are still sturdy enough to be used by a fourth generation!

What we didn't have in 1962 was running water in the classroom. That meant a trip down the hall for water to mix easel paints, wash finger paint from small hands, and implement first aid. A preschool without a sink and faucet is like a kitchen without a stove.

Our bathroom was the women's room down the hall, which was old, fitted for adults, and lacked counters for mop-up jobs and diaper emergencies. In order to enroll, our three-year-old children needed to be toilet trained—no small task for a parent of a child with a language or hearing handicap. One of my saddest memories is that of my relationship with one mother who had not realized her child needed to be toilet trained for entrance and saw me as rejecting her very loveable little boy when a needed diaper change created a crisis for me. She had not understood that toilet training was a necessary prerequisite for our program because we did not have facilities for changing diapers.

April 1963: *Easter week. Joe arranged for painting the preschool classroom and upright piano a soft aqua selected by me. A new staff member, Bev, helped me make valances for the windows with circus motifs on cotton percale. The room had a facelift! Transformed from the color of brown paper bags to soft underwater green.*

Outdoor play

An outdoor play period was an important part of our daily program year-round. I described our first playground in a letter to my mother. *Our outdoor play area is an enclosed grassy area with swings, sandbox, climbing rope, balancing boards, and wheeled toys (but no cement path on which to ride them). The women's washroom serves as our preschool bathroom, and also as our only access to the playground. The door is left propped open to the outdoors when we are outside, minimizing privacy inside. I learned today to crawl around on the grass and find all the tiny parts of the hearing aid that Sammy pulled out of his ear when he was angry. If nothing else this first week, I have mastered the handling of hearing aids, what to do when they fall out, what to do when they whistle. Meanwhile, I am waiting for a key to the outside door to the bathroom as I was locked out with the children one day when someone closed it.*

In another letter: *I was pleased to be invited to return for a second year and am now considered a member of our regular staff. My work seems much easier since I now have a substantial amount of prepared material and increased self-confidence. There are now three boys and two girls in my class. Had a shock yesterday when a new little girl, Jane, was brought to my classroom. When I adjusted one hearing aid, I discovered she had been born missing one ear. Recent surgery had created a middle ear opening. She appears now to be responding to sound.*

Understanding our goals

Acoupedic Research, which defined our grant, provided partial confirmation for the hypothesis that, if hearing loss is identified early in life and hearing aids are then fitted to young children, language and speech can be stimulated and learned. A study then in progress at the University of Colorado Medical Center, based on identifying hearing loss in early infancy, later provided further confirmation.

Joe had instructed me to talk to the children as though they were not limited in hearing and to surround them with experiences that would enhance language development. I was asked to minimize opportunities to read my lips and to regard each child as a whole person, not a child with a specific degree of hearing loss. That was a good fit for me. I have always preferred to see young children in terms of their potential rather than their limitations. A child development point of view emphasizes patterns of growth and recognizes that a young child learns most effectively when she brings all systems to bear on the learning process—thinking, acting, and feeling. In order to understand the philosophy behind "a child development point of view," it is helpful to review briefly how early childhood education became an academic discipline.

Early childhood education has roots in many disciplines

Child development became a separate academic discipline on campuses in the 1920s, and emerged from the combined interests of schools of psychology and of education. It was a logical new focus at the beginning of the progressive education movement. Recognition of the importance of the early childhood years was inspired by Jean Piaget's work in Switzerland about cognitive development, the educational theories of John Dewey and others, and the work of Freud and his followers. The new academic field drew on many disciplines including psychology, education, pediatrics, psychiatry, linguistics, sociology, medicine, nursing, nutrition, physical education, and the arts. Winona Graham, in her book, *First Encounters, A History of Early Childhood Education in Colorado*, observed that when I began as teacher in the Acoupedic program, my preschool "became the first special education preschool program in the State with a child development point of view."

In the early decades of the twentieth century, preschools were established on many college campuses as training centers for students who would become qualified directors of such schools, for which "nursery school" was the favored term into the 1940s. These programs accommodated children two to five years old for five days a week. They opened in the morning, served lunch, and provided naps before children went home. Programs and staffs were funded by the universities, and tuition was paid by parents. The directors were often women with doctoral degrees, highly regarded on their campuses. As early childhood education centers multiplied on university campuses, a new concept of their function was suggested by educator Katherine Read. She perceived the preschool as a "laboratory for human relationships." We incorporated that idea into our preschool. We designed our program to offer therapeutic opportunities for children at play with each other, and to include many areas of academic disciplines.

During World War II, many women stepped into the jobs vacated by men who had gone to war, and there was a dramatic increase in the number of programs needed for young children of working mothers. Privately operated preschools multiplied across the country to accommodate a new large population. We were unprepared to provide the number needed of quality-trained early childhood educators, which remains true today.

What does the preschool teach?

The preschool curriculum includes art, music, literature, drama, science, mathematics (block building), agriculture (gardening), husbandry (care of animals), physical education, nutrition, and much more. When implementing a "child development point of view," the teacher becomes a facilitator with an emphasis on learning rather than "teaching." The teacher's job is to encourage learning by selecting equipment and materials, arranging the physical environment, planning the activities, setting the time schedule, establishing consistent limits for behavior, and providing a place where children are respected, loved, and safe. She is aware that young children learn best from activities they initiate themselves.

Materials and activities lay the foundation for language development, and the relationship with the teacher, according to James Hymes (University of Maryland) is "critical for developing a positive self-concept and a sense of trust in the child's suddenly enlarged world." In 1955, the title of his book, *A Child Development Point of View*, coined the phrase which from then on described early childhood curriculum based on the developmental patterns of learning identified by the Swiss psychologist Piaget.

Near the end of my first month, Alice approached me with an unexpected question. "When are you going to start doing . . . (she hesitated for words) . . . your 'thing'?" I was startled and wondered, what was my "thing"? Poking around a bit, I learned that my predecessor had used part of each preschool morning to assemble the group of children with scrapbooks containing pictures they found in magazines, cut out, and pasted in their book. Gathered in a circle on the floor together they practiced saying the word for each pictured object or action.

On the contrary, I used group time sitting on the floor together as an opportunity to share music, stories, and rhythms. A time to dance, not a time to name pictures from magazines. I wondered then, as I do now, how a picture of an elephant compares in a child's mind with a similar sized picture of a toothbrush. Small children are not characteristically good at sitting still, and stories that are visually acted out on a flannel board or with puppets and dancing to music are a better fit for them. I asked Joe if he shared Alice's concern. He said he was pleased with the way I was managing our group activities. Alice's question was my earliest clue that there would be moments in the future when I would feel like the stranger at the table with some speech pathologists and audiologists who were more inclined than I to favor a structured teacher-directed style.

Our children's specific problems with communication were addressed in a half-hour of individual daily therapy. In my early years in the preschool, limitations of space required that children be taken out of class one or two at a time. Some of the children responded to this as an unwelcome interruption. For example, there was the time when

Sammy threw his hearing aid on the grass outdoors while Alice, running in high-heeled black patent leather-sling-pumps, tried to corral him for therapy. In our new building, constructed in 1972, we designed multiple small rooms for individual therapy so that all of the children could go out for the same half hour. The children's hearing was monitored by our audiologist, and a clinical psychologist was available for parent counseling. Regular evaluations were done by an audiologist and a speech pathologist.

As my first year moved ahead I wrote: *I love the opportunity to work with a mix of adults as well as young children. Interacting with staff, parents, and graduate students makes the job in Lakewood seem dull by comparison. It is a joy to feel autonomous, have good equipment to work with, and help when I need it. Yesterday a neurologist from London and two women from Boulder Public Schools spent the morning observing. Today I took our two ducks to school and turned them loose on the playground, to the delight of the children. Our youngest little girl, Debbie, was fascinated by them and followed them all around the playground. After Christmas two new children will join our group.*

Helpers in the preschool

Seniors and graduate students who helped me over the years in the preschool enriched my life. I missed the opportunity to interact with that generation after I retired in 1982.

Fukiko from Japan was one of my early assistants. She came to the University to study audiology and work with hearing impaired children. She was placed with me to learn about young children and to enhance her English. She came from a culture that regarded young children, and how adults relate to them, very differently than I did. We had much to learn from each other. I delighted in her excitement about her goal to earn a doctoral degree. She would exult as she repeated to me her full name preceded by the title she hoped to earn, "Doctor." She was sponsored by a Denver woman who had just built a lovely Japanese home on Lookout Mountain and who hosted Fukiko frequently at her Denver apartment.

Over the years I had many wonderful student helpers. Only once can I remember a doctoral candidate storming out of our classroom indignant at "being expected to help with the demeaning work of a preschool teacher." She was expressing a widely held value that teaching young children is a low status activity. By contrast, I remember one day when I was ill at home, and Bob, our Chief of Audiology with a PhD from Northwestern University, and one of the kindest men I have ever known, took over part of the preschool morning class and dealt competently with one of the little boys who had an accident in the bathroom.

A clinician for each child's therapy session

In an academic clinical setting, children have a series of student therapists, each of whom is supervised by a staff member. Clinicians come and go as determined by class schedules and training requirements. One therapist may work for just two academic quarters with a child and then be assigned to another client, such change being made to broaden exposure to different kinds of problems. Some of the children's therapists were undergraduate seniors just beginning to engage in clinical work, some were experienced certified clinicians, and others were doctoral candidates. I was the one constant adult for our preschool children, and I developed an increased sense of responsibility toward each child. I provided continuity for their first educational experience. I also needed to be flexible in relating to the training requirements for our college students.

Two children, Billy and Julie, although they were enrolled in different years, serve as examples of how training needs could require me to exercise diplomacy and compromise. Billy was enrolled in our preschool for two years, with a series of changing clinicians. I was the one constant in his preschool mornings. I felt keenly responsible for time spent with him, his clinicians, and his mother. Typically on a home visit I invited the current clinician to go with me.

On the other hand, Julie was assigned to a PhD candidate for therapy. Parent counseling and home visits were part of that candidate's training program. Usually I was the senior member on a counseling team. I had to learn to modify my role as counselor in this relationship.

Billy

Billy suffered brain damage in a near-drowning incident in his backyard wading pool. He was a handsome boy with light-flecked brown eyes, a rich head of smooth brown hair, and a penchant for dressing in cowboy hat and boots. He enjoyed playing with other children but didn't talk to them or to me. He was with us for two years, and more than once in those two years a newly assigned clinician told me with great excitement that Billy had finally learned to recognize the color "blue." As I write this, I wonder why I never raised the question as to whether his problems with colors might relate to visual acuity rather than language. In any case, he loved to do almost everything and painted enthusiastically with many colors at the easel.

Julie

Julie was a slender blonde girl with long wavy hair, excellent coordination, and good balancing skills. She loved our outdoor equipment and to be physically active on our playground. Her fine and gross motor skills were age appropriate. She enjoyed mixing food colors to see what she could make, and used a variety of materials designed to invite discovery. She played cooperatively with other children and joined in activities with enthusiasm. Her clinician was one of our stellar Ph.D. candidates, and a senior faculty member was the supervisor.

20

1963-64 Second year with the Acoupedic Program

My life was growing increasingly complicated as my second year began. I was mother to three children in elementary and middle schools. I was a professional woman on a university campus, and the wife of a geologist beginning to fly on global wings. *Received letters from Warren in South Africa where he is attending UNESCO meetings and getting acquainted with other Antarctic geologists. Most recently he toured diamond mines in Kimberley. He writes that he bought me a 45 cent Zulu hat to wear when I garden, which ought to be the only handmade Zulu hat on Garland Street.*

October 12, 1963: *Tuesday I will take our ducks and large tortoise to visit our school. Warren is coming to take pictures which I plan to include with the article I am preparing for publication in the NAEYC Journal (National Association for the Education of Young Children). Fukiko continues to help me in the preschool but will soon move on to begin her apprenticeship in the Clinic. Another graduate student, from Berkeley, will replace her as my helper.*

Over Christmas break, I prepared more flannel board stories for the children than I would ever use. Children's literature and poetry have been a lifelong delight for me as I read to my own children and my kindergarten classes. Now, as teacher to hearing-impaired children, I needed visual tools to help the children process and understand the sequence of a story. Flannel board figures cut from colored felt provided characters and props for dozens of stories. The children helped arrange the pieces on the flannel board as we told each story, and eventually acted out the story itself. Puppets of several kinds helped to tell stories.

Christmas break also gave me an opportunity to prepare written materials explaining goals and expectations for observers and helpers, write a sample intake form for my initial interview with mothers, and prepare an outline for recording observations of children in the preschool. All of this was a precursor to later teaching academic classes.

We have just evaluated two boys for the preschool group. One an adorable four-year-old, John, who is probably headed eventually for Broadway–an irrepressible performer who loves an audience and sports a wonderful permanent grin with twinkling eyes. He specializes in hanging by his knees upside down on the jungle gym. He is hearing impaired. The second little boy is Bobby, newly fitted with hearing aids in both ears.

Bobby

Bobby was a muscular and energetic little boy who plowed through preschool activities with obvious enthusiasm. He was awkward at both fine and gross motor tasks but always cheerful and unconcerned about minor accidents. He particularly liked to drive the big red tractor on the playground and to build indoors with our large hollow hardwood blocks. In the interest of safety, the walls of his structures were restricted to the height of two blocks. Sometimes he liked to play at the sink in the housekeeping center washing dishes.

A memorable event occurred outdoors the day I brought our ducks to school. We had long narrow hardwood boards that we could place on triangular stands to practice balancing skills. In his moving-man mode, Bobby decided to take one board off its metal base. The board wobbled in his grip and grazed the leg of one of the ducks resulting in a broken leg. The ducks were my daughter's pets, so I hastened to repair the damage. On my way home, I stopped at a veterinarian's office, and a splint was placed on the duck's leg. Our duck was the only one on our suburban street with a splinted leg. My daughter, Kathy, was very forgiving.

In January to my mother: *An exciting new development in our adjoining wing— the Child Study Center. David Elkind is the new director this year and is apparently becoming a close pal of Joe's. Dave graduated with his doctoral degree from UCLA last year before coming to DU. The new Chairman of the Department of Psychology hails from UCLA, your alma mater and Warren's. Dave has a fellowship to study with Piaget in Switzerland next year. I am going to take his class in Advanced Child Psychology next quarter which will meet at 11:40. Now that I'm beginning to use my tuition waiver to take classes, I plan to explore the possibility of working toward a graduate degree. It is important to do so if I want to continue us staff/faculty on a university campus.*
The Department of Sociology accepted me as a graduate student with an emphasis on the sociology of the family, and gave me credit for the graduate level course work I had taken earlier.

Artists at work

That'll be 50 cents

Doctor at work

23

How do we look?

Dressing up

Dinner time

Mommie at work

Lady at sink

Can you help wash up?

Inside the one-way mirror

Eensie weensie spider

goes up the waterspout

What do you do with these sticks?

Beat the drum loudly

What happens if I do this?

Rocking the boat

Large hollow hardwood blocks

Unit blocks build an airport

Visiting ducks

Going my way?

Hello mister turtle

26

Climbers

Parallel play

Measuring sand

Truckers at work

27

Helping each other

Swinging takes concentration

Hey, this is a big job!

Improvising outdoor play

Carpenters

Flannel board and hand puppets

Creating a story

Pilot study of physical education

Chapter Three
Broadened Horizons

A new population, a graduation, and a tent city

An ending and new beginning

The Acoupedic research was completed in late 1964, and Joe left the University. There followed an interim director in our Clinic whose name I no longer remember. My only encounters with him were when he popped his head through the preschool door to assure me that he wanted me to continue developing the preschool program, and that he was working to increase my salary! About this time I realized that I had settled for a salary that was not commensurate with my contribution to the clinic services.

David Elkind returned from studying with Piaget, and established a cooperative preschool in his wing of our aging building. He planned to apply for a federal grant and begin development of a model child study center. His grant proposals, however, were delayed in the administrative process. Discouraged, Dave left DU, moving first to the University of Rochester and then to Tufts University where he did establish a child-study center and earned an international reputation as a distinguished researcher, author, and child psychologist.

I continued to operate what became a preschool for children with "communication disorders." I was now a permanent member of staff, although for several more years my appointment was part-time. We enrolled hearing impaired children but expanded the preschool population to include those with other reasons for delayed language development. By the spring of 1967 seven children were in my morning preschool class. One had suffered a brain injury, one had a surgically repaired cleft palate, one had an articulation problem, and four had hearing losses. One little girl who joined the preschool haunts my memory.

Vonnie

Vonnie came to us initially for treatment as a hearing impaired child.

When I met her I learned that the audiologists were not able to determine the degree of her hearing loss, so she was not fitted with hearing aids. She seemed to be "too deaf to be deaf." She was small and athletic, with age-appropriate motor skills. For the year she was with me, she was a "loner" in the midst of the other children and engaged in solitary play, never uttering a word or sound. She was active but not aggressive. I never saw her smile. There was only one moment when I thought she responded to something I said. She was at the housekeeping sink washing dishes, when I noticed that her shoe lace was untied. It was my practice to talk to the children as though they heard everything. I said, "Vonnie, let me tie your shoe." She stuck her leg up, I tied the shoe, but now I wonder if I imagined it. Did that really happen? Nothing similar ever took place again in her year with me.

Vonnie's story was so painful for me that I was moved to bracket it in my memory with blank verse and to wonder what the limits to helping might be.

> A tiny blonde girl
> carried to our door
> > vomit stained pink dress
> > flushed cheeks surprised by fresh pox
> > delivered to school in her mother's arms
> expecting to stay.

> Three years old
> does not talk
> > too deaf to be deaf
> > school an island of hope
> sent back to her cage
> a sick little sparrow.

> Last night
> she drowned
> > five new kittens
> > quietly
> > one at a time
> in the basement bath.

Vonnie's parents were divorced. She lived with her mother and several older siblings. Her mother drove her to school five days a week. Her mother was a large woman. I first realized she had been pregnant with another child when I made a home visit and met her new baby. She led me to believe at that time that she had delivered the baby herself at home. No other information was offered. Vonnie's father was a trim, cooperative, well-dressed man who was asked to talk with us when we became alarmed about Vonnie. As per our recommendation, Vonnie and her parents began counseling and therapy at a local mental health center.

New staff, new faculty, new programs

In 1965, Jerry was hired as our new director. He was an audiologist, with fine credentials in aural rehabilitation, and the author of a celebrated textbook. He promptly added two women to our faculty in Speech Pathology, both of whom quickly became my close friends and enthusiastic supporters of my preschool program. Karol came from the University of Kansas, and Antje from Purdue University. The following year two senior faculty were added—Dan from the University of Kansas to fill a new role, Chief of Speech Pathology, and Bob from Northwestern University to be Chief of Audiology. With the addition over two years of these four faculty, one of the most satisfying times of my professional life began.

The new faculty members were enthusiastic about my preschool program which espoused what James Hymes (University of Maryland) defined as a "developmental point of view," but our new director, who preferred lip reading and sign language instruction, was uneasy with our multi-sensory normal-child approach.

Winona Graham, whose book *First Encounters* was mentioned earlier, adds this regarding my preschool: "Programs heretofore for children with special needs had been scattered and sporadic and ranged from expensive private treatment centers for various handicaps to the state-supported community centers for mental retardation. The University of Denver's Speech and Hearing Center offered preschool education for over twenty years with early childhood specialist Alicita Hamilton teaching the children with communication disorders."

Although I was aware that our director was baffled by my ideas, we had a positive relationship. I understood that he was anxious for community approval of every aspect of our program. His expertise was in aural rehabilitation for hearing impaired adults. He was sensitive to the fact that in the professional community of "teachers of the deaf" there were strong convictions about teaching methods and criticism of our earlier Acoupedic Program. Teachers of the deaf subscribed either to lip reading or sign language training, with a focus on visual and tactile clues, as opposed to our multi-sensory normal-child approach. Jerry was generous in his acceptance of me as the "stranger" on our faculty, from a totally different discipline. When I had surgery in 1966, his wife delivered a dinner for my family to my suburban home.

The speech pathology faculty invited me to move to their wing of the building that coming fall to develop a preschool program for children with "communication disorders." I wrote to my mother: *The new room has a low sink and running water where children can wash their hands, and I can mix paint and art materials. It does not have an observation booth nor a one-way mirror. For a while I am no longer in a goldfish bowl. I have an office adjoining the preschool classroom with shelves for my growing professional library, and my own telephone. The outdoor playground is a bit scruffy, with very little grass and much hard dirt. We share this with the new cooperative preschool in the Child Study Center, where two of the teachers are good friends of mine. We hope for a better playground when we start construction on a new building.*

We are winding up this year with a picnic for children, mothers, staff and clinicians at 11 o'clock. During our Spring Quarter we took field trips to the zoo, the natural history museum, several parks and playgrounds with mothers as helpers. The director of a new Speech and Hearing Center in Dallas, Texas called this morning asking to send a teacher up to observe me for a week. I am pleased and flattered at the prospect. She was told my preschool was one of the finest in Colorado!!!!

Over the summer our director, Jerry, hired a teacher of the deaf to join the audiology faculty and operate the program for deaf children. The new teacher began in my old room with the one way mirror. Within the first several weeks she moved her desk out to a small therapy room for an office, and turned over the operation of the daily preschool to graduate students in audiology

Good publicity

December 16, 1967: *Karol tells me I have "blossomed," which I think means I show greater self-confidence. I am certainly happily challenged by my work. My full time appointment has been approved by the Chancellor of the University and the Dean of Arts and Science. My article "A Preschool for Hearing Impaired Children," published in 1966 in Young Children, the journal for the National Association for the Education of Young Children (NAEYC), served to establish my credentials.*

I will begin working full-time instead of part time, teaching two half-day preschool sessions with younger children in the morning, older ones in the afternoon. It will be something of a push for me to do this while I finish my research and defend my thesis for a degree in the sociology of the family, but I have found that a part-time job automatically converts itself to a longer day without commensurate compensation.

Update on our family news: Warren's on a trip to the ancient city of Samarkand and will go to Siberia. He will visit a Russian kindergarten and take pictures for me. We expect him home via Brussels on December 20th."

Missy Hamilnook graduates

For several years I took courses in sociology, psychology, and education. This added a heavy load to my work, although I spread it out by taking one course per quarter. I drove two congested freeways each day to get to work. When I was enrolled daily in an 8 a.m. class in Abnormal Psychology one of the two freeways was under construction. Before leaving home, I fixed breakfast and packed sack lunches, although increasingly my three children could choose from the weekly cafeteria menus when they preferred to eat there. Our professor was annoyed that a few of us were sometimes a few minutes late to class, slowed by highway construction. So one morning he locked the classroom door at 8:01 leaving several of us outside for the hour. Thereafter, in spite of what I had to accomplish at home with my family before class, I managed to be prompt!

I spent the summer of 1967 doing research for my thesis. Warren was off doing field work in the central Idaho wilderness, and my teenage children had local jobs. I did a comparative study of the family role concepts of two groups of preschool children, interviewing and tape recording conversations with twenty children in a Head Start program and twenty children in a privately owned preschool. We were generously provided a private room for our conversations at each center. At each school, teachers selected ten boys and ten girls from their classes to talk with me. For each interview, I sat with a child at a small table and played with a doll family of five—father, mother, boy, girl, baby—and a few pieces of doll furniture. My standardized questions regarded tasks and roles within a family. I analyzed the tape-recorded interviews at home. I defended the completed 100-page thesis before a committee of three faculty members, two from sociology, one from psychology. By May1968, my degree work was completed and I was ready to graduate.

May 10, 1968. The thesis is polished, submitted and accepted. The orals are over and I am numb. Graduation comes next and my Director has asked the Dean to promote me now to full faculty status with a salary increase. The family has survived the ordeal of putting mama through college. I am so glad you plan to attend my graduation. Warren, Kathy and Jim will be there too.

After the celebration is over, we will get ready to take off for our second summer of camping through Europe. As we did in 1960, we'll rent a British van in London. This time we will head across the Channel to France, Switzerland, Italy, Greece and Yugoslavia. Larry will join us for part of the trip, leaving us in Sorrento to meet a college friend and climb Mont Blanc. He will rejoin us in Zermatt after climbing in the Swiss Alps–probably some mountain other than the Matterhorn as he considers that "too camp" for his climbing repertoire. I shall probably always be nervous and anxious about his devotion to climbing and certainly about being unable to communicate with him while he is off in France. He will carry his worldly goods in a backpack and travel by train from Sorrento to Chamonix.

Warren's global travels and Larry's climbing adventures were long before the days of cell phones and e-mail. I was often an anxious wife and/or an anxious mother left incommunicado. There was no way to talk to Antarctica except through short-wave, and none at all to a son climbing mountains.

Settling down in a new room

September 20, 1968. Now really established in my office, I made and hung valances at the windows in lieu of curtains. I pasted cut-outs of block shapes at the back of our open toy shelves so that our routine of putting unit blocks away could double as a perceptual training task. The children for this year arrived on Monday. The three-and-four-year olds come in the morning. In the afternoon there are five boys, five and six years old. It has been suggested that most of the boys show signs of autism. If true, that would make my preschool a singular Center!

October 12, 1968: *Have had a hectic week in my new classroom working with a four-year-old boy who is not yet toilet trained, a hearing-impaired girl with a heart defect, a partially-sighted little boy, and a brain-injured boy, details of injury yet to be learned. My immediate concern is to develop a learning plan for him. On Monday we will enroll three more new children in the morning preschool group following evaluation. That will mean an enrollment of thirteen in my two classes!*

As I continued to develop new ways to enhance the education of our preschool children, I also became caught up in the exigencies of the civil rights movement and the development of Head Start programs. Our small preschool world was impacted by changes in the national scene.

Civil rights upheaval

The Civil Rights Act of 1964, passed under President Johnson, changed the story of early childhood education forever. Awareness was raised about the condition of families who live in poverty. We discovered the poor child. When Sergeant Shriver, director of the Office of Economic Opportunity, initiated a new program called Head Start, a whirlwind of activity was loosed in Colorado. Early childhood educators mobilized to train new teachers, formulate licensing requirements for centers, and look sharply at issues related to public welfare. I became a founding member of the Colorado Association for the Education of Young Children (CAEYC), an affiliate of the National Association (NAEYC), served for three years in a tiered presidency, presented workshops at state and national meetings, and established the first CAEYC scholarship for a teacher of young children. The scholarship was funded by a book, *Colorado Gold*, which I compiled and edited.

Referrals to our university preschool program began to reflect the Head Start movement, and provided the opportunity to give our students experience working with different kinds of families. Antje, who did much of our intake evaluation of children at that time, was just the person to respond to the challenge. After she met four year old Susie, she told me in her most winning way that "Susie needs you." Now how could I resist that?

Susie

Susie and her mother, Sally, were able to ride the bus to our Clinic. Sally usually spent the morning in our waiting room and was available for conversations with staff while Susie attended preschool and speech therapy. Sally was referred to us by Denver's Department of Social Services, and was supported with welfare assistance and food stamps.

Susie had a heart-shaped face, pale puffy cheeks sprinkled with tiny brown freckles, wide-open pale blue eyes, and voice, articulation, and vocabulary of a much younger child. She was four years old and lived with single-parent Sally. Susie needed a good preschool program, and Sally needed help on many levels. We hoped that we could expand Susie's world with new relationships and interests as she increased her communication skills.

Sally had dark circles under her eyes, was painfully thin, and needed encouragement to take better care of herself and to improve nutrition for both of them. She needed help understanding Susie's needs as well as her own, planning meals, and finding activities they could enjoy together. In bits and pieces, I learned that Susie and Sally shared a bed, so one goal became to encourage Sally to move Susie out of her bed and into a small nearby bed of her own. A room of her own was not an option. I guessed that there might be a connection between Susie's baby-like behavior and their sleeping arrangement. In time, Susie did move to her own small bed.

I knew that I was getting through to Sally regarding nutrition and healthy meals when she called me one evening at my home (as I was cooking dinner) to ask if I could give her a recipe for stuffed bell peppers! That became a classic story for my parent counseling class. Our work with Susie and Sally was one of our truly satisfying efforts.

As we broadened our selection of children, a whole world of new experiences opened for us. Our ideal had been to try to achieve a balance in our preschool groups by selecting a mix of boys and girls, children with differences in presenting problems, and a balance of personalities that would maximize learning within the group. The reality of placement was that we accepted those who needed us most, with the chief restriction that we limited class size to six or eight children. What we actually had in some years was anything but an ideal mix. Many referrals began to include children of varied ethnicity and social class. Jose and Rubio were among those referred to us who may have taught us more than we taught them.

Jose and Rubio

Jose and Rubio needed help with communication. They lived in "The Projects," government-subsidized housing. Social workers arranged for them to be driven to and from our preschool program by taxi. I sometimes talked with their mothers by telephone. There was little opportunity for parent counseling and interaction. I had not yet started regular home visits.

They were active bright-eyed little boys with a strongly developed sense of mischief, few social skills, and very few words in English. They joined our preschool group with delight and energy. One noon I received a distraught call from Jose's mother: "Meesus Hamilton! What hoppened?" I had no idea what had "hoppened." It turned out that the two little boys arrived home stark naked having thrown their shoes and clothes out the taxi window in a hilarious ride back home. Loss of shoes and clothes was serious, and the family was helped to replace the lost items. I do not know how much their brief year with us changed their lives. They were certainly a bright spot in mine.

Marlene

Antje again informed me that she had a little girl who "needed" me. I shall never forget Marlene and her brother, mother and grandmother. She was a loveable, nicely dressed four-year-old with a haircut like that of Julie Andrews in Sound of Music. My first awareness of Marlene was hearing a little girl's shattering screams from a long way down our corridor. She was certainly not ready for our preschool program on her first visits to our clinic. Antje wrought her magic, and a few months later Marlene was ready to join the preschool group—another little girl to love and haunt my preschool memories.

Marlene was referred to us by a church social worker. Her older brother attended a private school in Denver. Marlene lived during the week in an apartment with her grandmother and grandfather who drove her to our clinic. She was a lonely, frightened little girl, and our first and continuing goal was to establish a warm, close relationship with her. We hoped expressive language would come with increased security.

Marlene was small and slender with a deceptive look of frailty. Her fine and gross motor skills were appropriate for her age, and she enjoyed our playground. She didn't talk with me or with other children, but by the time she joined our class she no longer screamed at us. What her early years had been like I have no idea, which was often the case with our children. She separated from her grandmother on her first morning at the preschool without incident and seemed eager to join us. She never developed special friendships with other children, but with time engaged in a variety of activities alongside them. Her grandmother worried that when we went outside each day to play, our sandbox might harbor germs. We did use a protective cover when not in use.

Sand, water, and mud are considered basic outdoor tools for the play of young children. Books have been written on the subject. At that time our sandbox was the only place for digging outdoors. We did not yet have a small garden.

A good early childhood program is committed to daily outdoor play, weather permitting. It is an integral part of experiential learning and a wonderful opportunity for children to engage in movements using their large muscles running, jumping, balancing, and climbing. Dressing to go outdoors provides an opportunity to encourage the child's ability to help herself. Self-sufficiency is a primary goal, and getting ready with coats is an important learning task. We used various tricks to help with that.

Marlene's grandmother was not the only parent concerned about winter outdoor play. Mothers reasonably worried about colds, and were anxious to know that we dressed children warmly. We dressed them in the clothes parents provided, and added supplements from our own reserves as needed. Boots, mittens, and snow-suits in cold weather, and we had extra mittens and caps in reserve. Putting shoes inside boots with feet that have outgrown last year's boots can be labor-intensive. Preschool teachers keep plastic grocery sacks that help slip shoes into tight boots.

A home visit

About this time I began a regular program of visits to the preschool children's homes. These visits were intended to be an informal way to get acquainted with a child's family and to allow the child to see her "teacher" in her home setting. I often invited the child's clinician to join me. On this occasion, it was the supervisor of therapy who went with me. The visit was memorable.

Marlene's older brother, about nine years old, had been kept home from school for this "special" occasion. While we adults were chatting, he disappeared briefly to "wash my car," as he proudly announced when he rejoined our group. Our three way adult conversation continued on for a bit with brother now smoking a cigarette at my elbow. Suddenly his mother said in a loud voice, "Haven't I always told you never to let me see you smoking!" He extinguished his cigarette. We left shortly thereafter.

Our plan for Marlene was centered on giving her a happy, busy, healthy morning with a group of other children her age and with adults who respected and treasured her. I could offer daily support and information to her grandmother, but chose to allow her Family Service agent and Antje to carry the counseling work. An important lesson for me as an early childhood educator was to know when to step back. I hope that worked for Marlene.

I learn to lecture

Fall 1969: *I think that I'm slowly becoming better at giving a lecture—at least I'm getting more practice. Last week I was asked to talk with our graduate students in Jim's class about "discipline" with young children. Unfortunately I was not aware that when I leaned on the podium I jiggled it. Jim quietly moved up to put a folded paper under one corner to balance the table. I was both embarrassed and grateful. Hopefully, I will learn to be more relaxed so that I pay attention to what I'm doing. Jim is generous to let me practice in his class. In November I am scheduled to speak to*

Head Start teachers, their aides, and the parents of their children about how children develop a self-concept. Then a talk in Dan's class on the relation of cognitive growth to language development.

We are in the early stages of planning a year's research with our morning preschool group on the relation between acquisition of motor skills and language development. A doctoral candidate from the Department of Physical Education will be working with me. We hope to share our work at the end of the year at conferences, workshops, and in a professional journal.

Jumping, climbing, balancing, and catching balls

In the fall of 1969, we began a pilot program in our morning preschool class. Pride, a doctoral candidate in the Department of Physical Education at DU, worked with me to plan what we would do. She would come two mornings a week during the school year to join our class and emphasize movement education. She brought balls, bean bags, tumbling mats, walking boards, inner tubes, ropes, and ladders to use in our classroom and on our playground. On several occasions we went to the campus gym where there were climbing bars and a trampoline. Pride engaged with each child individually to perform a variety of balancing tasks and to develop motor competence. Winter Quarter, we added time at the University swimming pool with the children's mothers joining us in the water.

Pride selected equipment and tasks. Before starting the project she had reviewed the research regarding motor skills of normally developing and at-risk preschool children. Young children with developmental problems often are chronologically behind in motor competency—some are several years behind. Our pilot study proposed to see what might be helpful for our children.

It was my task to accompany action with narration, and to comment about what the child was doing—jumping, climbing, balancing, throwing—including prepositions to emphasize spatial concepts related to the child's bodily movements. At that time, one of our doctoral candidates was studying the importance of prepositions in language acquisition.

What we planned to do was a good match for my philosophy. It fit with our goal for activities to stimulate language by adding casual non-judgmental narration as a child finger-painted, worked with clay, engaged in dramatic play, cooked, worked with blocks, or tended the gerbils and canary. But in this case we planned to place particular emphasis on physical activity and gross motor skills. Our goal was to enrich the child's receptive and expressive language through movement education.

Narration is an important, natural aspect of the development of language. Children learn receptive language skills as they listen and process what they hear. The best example of early language learning is the mother-child model. Most mothers narrate spontaneously what their child is doing, seeing, and sometimes feeling, and then expand on their child's utterances as they start to talk. I enjoy listening to a mother in the grocery store as she pushes her cart with seated young child past the fruits and vegetables and is talking about what they are seeing and buying.

Research by Hart and Risley, begun in the 1990s, about *The Power of Talking to Your Baby,* focused on the exposure of infants and toddlers to language spoken to them by parents and caretakers. The sometimes ridiculed stream of parent-to-infant-talk is actually very important, with large differences between families living in poverty and those who do not. Experiments are now being conducted with trained home visitors helping at-risk families learn to generate family conversation .

We kept daily written records of our project, with the help of our college students. Adults narrated actions stressing prepositions as a tool for emphasizing the child's concept of his body in space. For example, an adult would say as Eddie jumped on a large inflated tire on the ground: "Here, Eddie. Can you jump on this tire? Hey, look at you, you're jumping up and down." And, "Just look how high Eddie jumps! That's a good trick!" Eddie responded by telling us, "I ready to jump now. I jump. I know a trick!" Some of the children did not volunteer comments. We kept written records of activities and communication.

It was a good year to have outside help in planning an enriched program. Letter to my mother in October 1969: *Fifteen children are enrolled in the two preschool groups this fall. One four-year-old girl and fourteen boys. Some referred by the Department of Welfare, some by Head Start programs, and some by pediatricians at the University of Colorado Medical Center. One child is "apraxic" (has problems using muscles appropriate to saying words), several are "brain injured," one is said to be "psychotic," and several have "articulation" problems. Tomorrow we add a little boy who stutters. My work is challenging, and I go to bed exhausted.*

At the end of the year, Pride and I wrote a brief article about our work together for the *Journal of Health, Physical Education, Recreation* that was published in 1972. We also presented several local workshops and one at a state conference. Warren had taken photographs of us at work with the children so that we had colored slides (long before the advent of PowerPoint presentations) to illustrate our discussions. The chairman of the Department of Physical Education wanted us to apply for a grant to continue further research together, and was disappointed when I decided not to do that. The pilot study had begun as an experimental program, and Pride had done an outstanding job of planning and implementing many excellent tasks. But it was not something I wanted to be obligated to do in the coming year. I think she understood my decision.

Dan assured me that the choice was mine to make. A viable research project would require testing the children before, during, and at the end of the study. If our preschool group had been enrolled in a single all-day program, this would have been a golden opportunity to learn more about language as it relates to gross motor skills. However, our children came to preschool for two-and-a-half hours a day with half an hour out for individual speech therapy. Additional out-of-class time would mean either sacrificing time for children to play together or extra time for parents to bring the children in for testing.

Our program was not the right place to do this in the coming year, for the constraints on play time were not acceptable for a half-day program. In addition, the pilot study was teacher-centered rather than child-centered, and our teacher-centered experiment in the swimming pool had not gone well. Some of the children became frantic in the locker room when mothers began to help them into their swim suits. While water play at our table within the preschool setting was looked forward to, the strangeness of a large locker room, the need to change to a bathing suit, and the effect of the large pool were overwhelming for some of the children. The activity was time consuming, and did not enhance the preschool experience.

Naming the problem

I began to consider an issue that had long been at the back of my mind. Some children came to us with a diagnostic label, often only a tentative suggestion, from a previous evaluation at another facility. One year I had five little boys in my preschool who were referred because they were thought to be possibly "autistic." We were then only beginning to study autism in children, and these diagnoses, like many others, may have been premature.

I was uncomfortable about the impact of a label on a child's future and on family dynamics. It does help to know what is "wrong" in order to try to "fix" it, and a diagnosis calls for an intervention plan, but tentative labels may have long life spans. Does a diagnosis follow a child throughout his school career? Limit him, directly and indirectly? Can the problem become more important than the child?

Working with Joe and the hearing impaired children in my first years in the clinic, I concentrated on regarding each child holistically and optimistically. Observing a child playing freely in a familiar preschool classroom with other children provides a wonderful opportunity to revise and expand understanding of that child. The open preschool exposes more behavior over time for evaluation than does an individual testing situation, and I was delighted whenever invited to share my observations of a child with other professionals at a staffing. One staffing at Children's Hospital lingers in my memory.

Arnold

Arnie was five years old, and we needed to plan for public school placement as he finished his time with us. We suggested to his parents that an evaluation be done at Children's Hospital, and a referral was made with their consent. Following a series of tests, a meeting was arranged for his parents, our speech pathologist, and me to discuss the findings with the hospital staff. A pediatrician presided over our discussion, which was also attended by a psychologist, a social worker, and a physical therapist from the hospital staff.

We met in a comfortable room with upholstered furniture and small end tables, more like a living room than an office. I sat next to the parents on the couch, hoping that might offer them a sense of physical support. The pediatrician presented the findings of the assembled experts skillfully and gently.

Mother and Father had totally different reactions. Mother said with a smile and in a voice that sounded relieved, "Oh, I feel so much better now that I know what he is." She repeated to me later at school that she had understood at the staffing that Arnie was a slow learner. Sometimes naming a thing cuts it down to size, and suggests a solution.

Father said nothing. The pediatrician broke a prolonged silence and asked the father if he had any questions about what had been said. Father replied, "I haven't heard a word you said." He had been staring at the ceiling throughout. Denial is a common defense and sometimes a useful temporary tool in coming to grips with anxiety. There was more silence. When he could bring himself to ask, the father's question was "Will he grow up to be a 'man'?" The responses were optimistic and gentle. Arnie's father seemed to relax. Then we began to consider plans for Arnie's schooling. We agreed that he would enter his neighborhood public school on schedule, with extra help as needed. He returned to our preschool program for the remainder of the Spring Quarter the same happy, active little boy.

March 8, 1970. *Received an interesting job offer which I took under consideration over the weekend. I was asked to be Director of the Training Program for teachers and personnel in day care centers in the Denver metropolitan "target" areas. Funding is from the Model Cities Program, and my salary would have been twice my present one. The job would be fascinating and a marvelous professional experience. But it requires a twelve month contract and includes lots of evening meetings. I declined the offer on the ground that it was not the right time in my family's life to expand my calendar work year. My DU colleagues told me that they held their breath waiting for my decision. Nice to be wanted.*

Attended three days of national NAEYC meetings at the Brown Palace downtown. Topic: Open Education, The Legacy of the Progressive Movement. Had a wonderful visit with David Elkind, now at the University of Rochester and was invited to lunch with Roma Gans, emeritus from Columbia University. She is considered the "grand old lady of progressive education." I am hoping to attend several other conferences soon, one at Pacific Oaks in Pasadena, another with Jimmy Hymes in Salt Lake City.

By May 1970 an agitated national mood disrupted our campus life: While the preschool continues to chug along, the world has suddenly intruded on our college life and my personal life. On May 6th, the anti-Vietnam war movement erupted on our campus with the erection of a tent city which the students named "Woodstock West."

Woodstock West, a tent city

For long stretches of time it was possible to operate within the preschool setting as in a separate bubble of space. The children were loveable and responsive, their parents caring and involved, conditions that optimize the benefits of education. But the atmosphere of the late 1960s was pervasive, and change escalated throughout the 1970s, manifesting itself in several different ways on our campus.

Imagine that it is May 4, 1970. Ohio National Guardsmen shoot and kill four students at Kent State University, and wound nine others. The students are protesting the escalation of the Vietnam War. Fear and anger sweep campuses across the nation. My son, Larry, is a student in Santa Barbara at the University of California. His sister, Kathy, is at Smith College in Massachusetts. I am teaching at the University of Denver. My son, Jim, is in high school discussing the draft and the war with his classmates. The crisis becomes for me what the sociologist C. Wright Mills called "a public issue and a private trouble."

On May 6, about fifteen hundred DU students gather to "mourn their fallen comrades at Kent State." They form a picket line outside the Chancellor's office threatening a strike and boycott of classes. There is deep concern among our students and faculty even though our building is two blocks north of the center of disturbance. When the news hits the newspapers, we discontinue our clinical services, which include operation of the preschool.

On May 8, about 5,000 students and faculty attend a convocation, but it fails to quiet the students. Deciding to "build not burn" (rioting students in Santa Barbara had set fire to the Bank of America), students begin construction of Woodstock West, a disheveled village of tents and makeshift shelters built on a campus lawn, named to honor the peace theme of the protest held in 1969 in Woodstock, New York.

The population of the tent village fluctuates from several hundred to 2,000 inhabitants. There are debates, performances, speakers, and communal living and singing. One student describes it as a huge seminar with people wandering from tent to tent talking with each other. A fraternity house becomes the communications center. Militant activists arrive to join the student protesters. Two of the faculty men in our department join other faculty volunteers to walk the tent city at night in the interests of keeping the peace.

On May 11, two hundred Denver Police and forty State Troopers move students out of the shanty town and tear down their structures. Police arrest eighteen students and two faculty members (not ours!). The police leave, and the students retrieve the tents and building materials from the dump and build Woodstock West II.

The Chancellor announces the National Guard will have to be called. Governor Love visits the campus but no agreement is reached between administration and students. The students demand academic reform and construction of an outdoor public forum. The National Guard arrives early on May 13 with live ammunition, and find only one sleeping student in the evacuated camp. Tents and structures are torn down again, and this time carted away in dump trucks. Denver police patrol the campus to prevent another rebuilding.

The spring quarter has almost ended, and we close the preschool until the summer session begins. The conflict dies down over the summer.

Chapter Four
New Building and A Designer Playground

Before we can move

In the fall of 1970 campus life settled down to business almost as usual, although echoes of social change remained. The rebellion against the Vietnam War and the draft lottery was just one expression of the civil rights movement begun in the '60s. As we entered the 1970s, the women's movement was felt on our campus with issues of status and promotions. We had been jolted out of the complacency of our academic lives.

September 27, 1970: *This fall we opened preschool with "graduated entrance." We invited two or three children at a time to come with their mothers on different days to get acquainted with each other and with our routines. Warren helped me carry my goldfish bowl, gerbils in their cage, and boxes of books to school. He hung mobiles and repaired some toys. I scrubbed and defrosted the refrigerator. I set in a supply of non-perishable healthy snacks to accompany the children's daily milk. I will get fresh fruit each week. It's my responsibility to provide snacks; milk is delivered to our refrigerator.*

Thursday evening there was a picnic for faculty and students at a faculty home in the foothills. We made salad in a pickle barrel, and our hostess baked twenty pumpkin pies. We cooked hamburgers on the outdoor grill and drank hot buttered rum made with apple cider. Toward the end of the evening, a light rain began to fall as we sat around the outdoor campfire. There is a wonderful sense of unity and camaraderie among the faculty which is reflected by the students.

I'm still busy in the community. In addition to representing the Mental Health Association on the Board of Directors of the Jefferson County Mental Health Center, I am also writing a weekly column, "Worry Clinic Mailbox," for the Association, published in our local newspaper The Sentinel. It is a sort of "Dear Abby" column re mental health. So far I've had to invent my own questions and answers with back-up from my consulting professionals.

Alumni of our program began to solicit funds for our new building to be built at the south end of the campus. The architectural plans were ready and construction could begin soon. We could hardly wait to have our own building. Staff and parents would be able to sit behind one way mirrors to observe the children. We would have large observation rooms in which our academic classes could watch our faculty demonstrate techniques of working with adults. We planned to have new equipment for our audiologists, and video cameras to record the work of students and faculty.

More new challenges

February 20, 1971. *One of our graduate students asked me to guide an independent study for her next Quarter. Her topic is "Sociological and Psychological Correlates of Parent-Child Relations." I'm hoping that I can develop an outline for my graduate students in the parent counseling class that will emphasize the sociology of the family. It is important to help our students expand their understanding of a child beyond a "speech problem." I will give a lecture next week to students in the department of Physical Education describing last year's motor skill training program.*

September 28, 1971. *I returned to campus to learn that hard times have hit the University. Funds for promotions have been frozen. The Chancellor has promised to save our promotion money until the freeze is over, and I have another new assignment! I am to coordinate the work in our clinic of two graduate students from the School of Social Work. They will be with us for their first year of "field experience," details to be worked out. I guess I was chosen to serve as liaison since I now hold a degree in sociology. I am very uneasy about this as there are territorial issues for each of our faculty who have priority in working with our clients.*

I recognize now that I often increased my professional role and community commitments with more enthusiasm than wisdom regarding work load. Caught up in the excitement of our expanding academic program as well the hopeful idealism of the Head Start movement, I added too many new responsibilities. My thinking was that I'd have more time as my own children became more independent, and Warren's travels around the world had been increasing.

December 5, 1971. *Christmas break begins on Thursday. I am so grateful each December to have time to integrate the various parts of my life, but it's also a time to enjoy special festivities. Last Friday I invited the students in my counseling class to come to lunch at our home. The Clinic will have a Christmas party for faculty and students Wednesday evening. The preschool children and their mothers will go with me on Tuesday to the Denver Art Museum to see special Christmas exhibits for children, then back to the Clinic for a simple party. And so it goes.*

March 26, 1972. *Things go smoothly at the Clinic. It is fortunate because my thoughts are often drawn to Larry on the west coast and to Kathy on the east coast. Warren is in Persia this week visiting Tehran, Shiraz, Isfahan, and points in between. He has just finished time in Malaya where he was a keynote speaker in meetings at the University of Kuala Lumpur. In April he will give talks in London and Newcastle-upon-Tyne. Jim helps me maintain balance at home.*

I am disappointed in the way our new arrangement with the students from the School of Social Work is turning out. It is a big headache and probably won't be long-lived. They want to work independently with our clients without including our faculty, which just won't work for us. The inexperienced social-work students assigned to us are at the beginning of their academic study. Our clients have complicated needs. We take pride in our ability to provide counseling plus therapy, and we want to have close relationships with them. It isn't as though our clients require multiple counselors. Their supervisor is adamant that they handle "group work" by themselves. One of their men has a serious problem in personal hygiene about which Karol had the courage to confront him.

September 26, 1972: Back to the Clinic last Monday. All is chaos. I thought I had arrived at the "funny farm." The new building is almost ready for us but work has not yet begun on our new playground. Our director looks frazzled. He has not yet ordered new office furniture, so we move on Saturday at 7 a.m. with our old pieces which my buddy, Karol, calls "early Goodwill." I can't decide whether to laugh or cry.

Among our problems is that too many students were accepted for the coming year so we have been holding the large classes in my preschool classroom. Dan is our faculty star, attracting students from around the nation who are particularly interested in voice disorders and aphasia. Jim, added to our faculty at Dan's suggestion, works miracles for children and adults who stutter. So a whole gang of new students have come to participate in our speech pathology program. While my preschool classroom is used to accommodate enlarged classes, I try to work quietly in my office. I miss Antje who left us last year to get ready for a third baby. Her clinical skills and ability to work with young children, college students, and parents, plus her enthusiastic support of our preschool, enriched our program as well as my professional life.

A big moment for me. I was named "Volunteer of the Year" by the Jefferson County Mental Health Association. Connie was disappointed that I wasn't around to be honored at our annual meeting as Warren and I were off on a trip to western Pacific islands. Also was elected by the membership of CAEYC to their Board of Directors.

A designer playground

Earlier in the spring of 1972, I talked with our director about ideas for the new preschool playground. He was distracted by other matters. I assumed that he had decided against planning a playground, but as I was packing my books to leave for the summer in late May, he told me that funds had been found for construction.

Robert Utzinger, chairman of the Department of Architecture at the University of Colorado, had a distinguished reputation for designing creative preschool playgrounds. I had talked with him at a gathering of early childhood educators and knew he would work with us if invited to do so. Our director hired him to draw up a plan for us. He made a miniature architectural model of our playground for us to approve. We were delighted with his ideas. When Dan saw the model he laughed and said it would be fun to run tiny toy cars on the little bike paths.

September 1972: *The playground will have a cement path for tricycles and a large circular sand area below a grassy hill with built-in slide. At the other end of the yard will be another grassy square for swings and sturdy metal climbing frames to hold moveable balancing boards. Dividing the two halves of this upper area will be a slightly raised wooden deck with a small roofed area for shade and picnic tables—I shall call it our "teahouse of the August moon."*

Warren will mount a steering wheel and small wooden propeller for airplane play on the railing of the extended deck. There is a shallow circular cement lined pool for floating boats in the middle of the cement tricycle path which is a "round-about" for circling bikers. Below the deck and on the lower side of the grassy knoll there will be a three tiered area for planting radishes, pumpkins, and sunflowers—our "hanging Babylonian garden." A slide will be set in the ground at the top of the hill. There will also be a place on the fence in the lower area to build a hutch for a rabbit if we wish to do so. A high wooden fence will enclose the grounds. Railroad ties and short round posts in graduated heights will define spaces and provide opportunities for climbing and balancing. It is going to be perfectly wonderful!

Actual construction of the playground began in late summer and was completed in the fall. For a while we had to improvise outdoor play for our children at a nearby park.

October 1, 1972: *As I watch the workers build our playground I am concerned that our doors do not open at ground level. Our single exit door for the southwestern preschool classroom opens to a cement porch with five steps down and only metal railings and a low cement wall separating us from a grassy plot twenty feet below. The clinical arm of the Department of Psychology is lodged in our basement. Understandably, they wanted large windows for office light and that meant elevating the building. The good news is that there will be storage with doors under our steps which can be padlocked for outdoor moveable play equipment.*

We're going to have to be very careful supervising the children when we use those steps. I had hoped we would have doors which would open from the classroom directly to the playground so that in good weather children could move from indoors to outdoors in their play. I wasn't privy to the architectural details of the preschool classrooms as they were developed and, of course, was off campus for the summer. Obviously, now it is a matter of accepting a done deal. Fortunately, the exit door is too heavy for small children to open. It is going to be such a wonderful outdoor space that we will just have to learn to cope safely!

New building, new department

Moving into our new quarters was both exciting and challenging. We became officially a separate academic department of the University. In addition, we continued our historical function, since 1942, as a speech and hearing clinic, providing services to the community.

To my delight, we had two large sunny preschool classrooms on the south end of the main floor—one for hearing impaired children in the southeast corner, and one for my group of children with "communication disorders" in the southwest corner. The long wall of my room faced west to the Rocky Mountains with two large floor-to-ceiling windows and two tall narrow windows to the south overlooking our playground. It was a room filled with light.

At the bottom of the windows were low stone shelves covering heating units, ideal for holding pots of bright red geraniums. Our college students told me that looking up at the flowers in our windows gave a cheerful bright beginning to their mornings. The low stone heating units, on which the flower pots sat, also warmed the floor in winter for children engaged in block play and teachers sitting beside them. Part of the floor was carpeted, and part was a washable surface for easy mop-up of spills from art and from water-table projects with sand and water.

There was a large open bookcase of shelves for unit blocks, wooden trucks, toys, and puzzles. Seashells, magnets, leaves, and visiting small animals in cages could share the top shelf below the large one-way mirror concealing an observation room. Children's paintings were framed and hung on a floor-to-ceiling cork wall. There was a housekeeping center for dramatic play in one corner, and an all-purpose table and eight small chairs in another. There was a nook with colorful cushions for quiet time with a book.

Parents, students, and visitors had two choices for observing classroom activity. We had a large observation booth with sound system behind the one-way mirror at the north end of the room. I had a pleasant office off the classroom with a second window overlooking the playground, and bookshelves to house my professional library, and a smaller one-way window in my office faced the room from the east. I could encourage and guide observations from both places.

Storage space for extra preschool materials and equipment was available in a room between the two preschool classrooms. But what we didn't have was a child-size sink with faucet and a utility sink for mixing paints. However, I was so thrilled with everything else about our new quarters that I told Dan I could cope and "didn't mind." He predicted, "You will," and he was right.

Neither was there a bathroom with child-size fixtures on the first floor. Our preschool children had to share the public restroom for women. There was no counter space around the wash basins, only adult height wash stands and several stalls. There were no surfaces or cupboards to accommodate first aid needs which might arise. We quickly bought step stools for children to stand on to reach the basins. It was a large room that could have accommodated facilities for children on one side. Lack of separate child-size facilities was an unfortunate oversight for both adults and children, and I still wonder how licensing requirements could have been ignored.

I relied on my camping skills to solve the hand-washing problem. I was not about to give up easel painting, finger painting, and work with clay, paste, and other messy creative materials. I set up a small table covered generously with oilcloth, bought a plastic bowl for clean water, and a pitcher to hold fresh water. Under the table I placed a large bucket in which to pour used water. Dumping used water and fetching fresh water was a four times-a-day chore mostly for me. Sometimes student aides helped, but they had tight schedules between their classes and therapy. Hygienic and janitorial matters often become the responsibility of teachers in charge.

As we began 1973 in our new building, we continued to enroll three, four, and five-year-old children. The younger children came in the morning, the older ones in the afternoon. Each class was limited to eight who needed speech therapy for half an hour each day. Our college students worked one-on-one with a child, each supervised by a faculty or staff member watching through a one-way mirror. To the great disappointment of our staff, who had long dreamed of individual therapy rooms with one-way mirrors, the therapy rooms were so small they resembled closets. Any child or therapist with claustrophobia was challenged. Antje, who liked to have space to work informally at a child's level on the floor when appropriate, would have been dismayed by those small therapy cubicles.

The children

Despite frustrations that surfaced with settling in, the children continued to make our days rewarding and interesting. They were loveable, each with a distinctive personality—able to teach us so much as we interacted with them. Wilma and Michelle were in our new groups.

Wilma

Wilma was a tall, slender five-year-old. She had very short, curly brown hair with a tiny clip-on bow, large observant brown eyes, and skin the color of cinnamon. She was casual about engaging in activities but slowly expanded her choices. Her clinician aptly described her to me as having "two speeds—slow and stop." She was disinterested in conversation with other children and adults. She was enrolled in the afternoon group, and participated in many of the indoor and outdoor activities. Her mother visited with me frequently and wanted to help us as we worked with Wilma. During her year in the preschool, Wilma never really engaged in conversation with adults or children, but her vocabulary increased as she worked with her therapist.

Michelle

Three-year-old Michelle was carried in to preschool on her first day dressed in party clothes—an organdy dress, new black patent leather shoes and white socks with ruffled lacy edges. She had golden brown curls and wore a serious expression. It was obvious that she was a loved little girl. Anticipating that she might be anxious separating from her mother, we invited her mother to stay with us for a number of mornings. At my suggestion, she brought a book to read on the second morning. On succeeding days she moved her small chair and book to a far corner of the room. Separation at the preschool door was achieved without tears following this gradual withdrawal. Michelle came to school after her first morning dressed in attractive comfortable play clothes suitable for playground sand and slide.

Michelle was with us for two years, and blossomed as she developed varied interests, played happily alongside other children, and became increasingly independent and self-sufficient. Her mother relaxed as she saw that Michelle was supported by warm, caring adults and was accepted at play with the other children. During her time with me I never heard Michelle talk to other children, nor did she talk with me. I would love to know about her journey after she left us.

As an undergraduate at Scripps College, I learned from my mentor, Molly Mason Jones, to set three all-encompassing goals for preschool children: 1) to have happy, satisfying relationships with others; 2) to develop a variety of interests; and, 3) to accept willingly those things which have to be done. Michelle in her years with us seemed to achieve those three goals, although without talking with us.

Parents learn from parents

Just as our preschool philosophy recognized that children learn from each other, we found that our parents interacting in regular group meetings also learned from each other–a wonderful experience for me. At our group meetings, conversation took on a life of its own after a topic was selected for discussion. I could provide materials, then the mothers would take over—sharing, advising, supporting, and sometimes contradicting each other. I found that I could almost always depend on someone in the group to counter a misconception. My role was to arrange the meetings and provide resources as needed. Occasionally, we had a potluck dinner at one of their homes, including fathers and some of the children's clinicians.

February 1973: *Somehow the same job held over multiple years expands with time. I think that's a rule but I haven't heard it articulated. This year I am invited to be a participating lecturer in two of our introductory academic classes. Meanwhile, I'm still responsible for our graduate level Parent Counseling class one Quarter each year. This means that I have had to prepare more lectures and select more text materials. I am stretching myself thin but have to admit that I love doing it all and do have the long break at Christmas as well as the summer months for preparation.*

Teaming with student helpers

Teaming with student helpers was a major responsibility. As my experience increased, the information I wanted to share with them expanded. I began to try to meet with them as a group as often as possible, and developed an informal handbook of preferred laboratory practices. Time commitments made it almost impossible for students to meet with me individually, and I was not asked to evaluate them. Our first discussion always began with how to give directions to children when it became necessary to do so. Ideally, a teacher tells a child what to do rather than what not to do. For example, if Tommy is squirting the water from his syringe at Joe, the adult's response should be something to the effect of "Water stays in the water table" (as Tommy's syringe is aimed by the adult back to the water). Not, "Don't squirt water at Joe." I prepared a sheet of exercises with negative sentences. When we met for training discussions, I asked them to re-word the statements for practice.

Another important instruction was to get down at eye level to listen and talk with a child. Eye contact is very important in establishing a relationship. In my parent counseling class, I often used an exercise in which students were paired together, one sitting on the floor one standing tall, to carry on a three minute conversation, then changed places, to simulate the experience of a small child in an adult world. In conscientiously following my own good advice about squatting to establish eye contact over more than twenty years, I found (as did my college mentor) that repeated deep knee bends may be great exercise but can lead to knee replacements in later years! And that leads me to why you find me on the floor listening and talking with Tim as he builds a structure with blocks.

Tim

Tim was four years old when he enrolled in our morning program. He was a particularly loveable blue-eyed blonde boy with a small tuft of soft hair that stood up at the top of his part. He loved our hardwood unit blocks and played mostly by himself. We had wooden cars of several sizes, the middle size being his favorite. He repeatedly used the blocks and car to create a very particular drama with himself as director—a car driving through a car-wash. For weeks this continued. When I joined him on the floor, I learned what his structure was and what the car was doing. One day when we were so engaged, Tim glanced out through our large window and commented on a small yellow car in our parking lot with unusually large round headlights. He commented "that car is watching us—it has big eyes."

Tim's young, attractive mother cared deeply about him and was troubled about several aspects of his behavior. He often got up in the middle of the night to play records on his own phonograph in his bedroom, until he could be persuaded to go back to bed. I don't know to what extent he listened to the records or how much he was just enjoying watching them go around. He had a tendency to repeat an activity for long periods of time. The challenge became how to help him move on when that happened.

When I talked to his mother about the car-wash play, his mother told me that one of his favorite excursions with her was to drive through a mechanized car-wash. He was fascinated by the explosions of water jets and bombastic noise of air-drying. From that I guessed that in his block play he was trying to work through a mix of feelings and to understand the process. I found a way that I could join him and, without comment, extend his repetitious play by introducing a new prop—a toy gasoline pump. Sitting beside him, I placed it just beyond the car-wash. Soon Tim decided to fill the "tank" of the car and drive it "home." Together we built a garage for the car.

Tim's play with blocks and car illustrates the progressive stages of socio-dramatic play, and how these stages reflect maturation. He responded well to my unobtrusive extension of play, adding a prop to further his drama. He was using the typical patterns of a three-year-old when he engaged in make-believe in regard to objects, action, and situation. He was like a four-year-old in showing persistence developing a theme and in explaining his activity to an adult. What he didn't do was engage in play with another child. So that became one goal for Tim.

A number of four-year-old boys in our preschool were repetitious in their play until the scene was set to encourage new choices. For many children choosing to do the same activity over and over is merely a stage as they become comfortable in the school setting, and then they move on to play with other children or try something different. Ralph was one of those. In his early days with us he repeatedly headed for the playhouse. One of many therapeutic benefits of a preschool is that it can be a place where ideas and experiences can be worked out in play.

Ralph

Ralph selected our housekeeping center as his favorite spot indoors. He typically played there by himself, dressing up in props from our playhouse closet of clothes. At first he preferred the sequin dresses, feather boas, and hats with flowers, but then began to choose to pull our big work boots on over his shoes, don a brown jacket and top off the outfit with a man's felt hat for sartorial splendor.

Ralph was referred to us by the University of Colorado Medical Center. We were told that he was "apraxic"–that is, he had a neurological problem which made it difficult for him to use the muscles needed to say words. In professional language, he had difficulty with the volitional formation of speech. Ralph was tall, slender, and wore glasses. He was an energetic climber on our playground. His balance was good, his gross motor skills excellent, and his energy level high. He came eagerly to school and played cooperatively on the playground with other children. For example, he loved to roll balls down our slide for a friend to catch or send a bucket of water down to be received in another bucket by a playmate. He was a happy youngster with a challenging speech problem.

Our new classroom

Glued-wood sculptures

Art corner

The
beauty
parlor

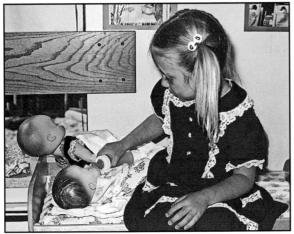

Doctors at work

Sewing buttons

Puzzles are hard

How much does it cost?

At the office

Chocolate pudding anyone?

Architects at work

Traffic accident in construction zone

Consultation

59

Mixing food colors

Bunny comes for a visit

Shells and sand

Hydraulic engineers

Siphoning water for dinosaurs in the sand

Halloween flannel board story

Halloween hand puppets

Story book

Orchestra

Finger plays

Autoharp

61

New building and playground

Upper level playground

Slide built into the hill

Sand area, lower level

Outdoor play on a snowy day

62

Making a lake in the sand

Joy in Motion

Bridge

Boat harbor

63

Wood working shop

Flat tire

Harvesting our garden's crops

See what I can do!

64

Off on the fire truck

Flying the airplane

Firemen to the rescue

Upper-deck crew at work

Hoisting with a pulley

Chapter Five
Living With Change

Delights and Challenges of A New Building

Spaces and people

So many of our dreams for the new building came true. We had rooms with one-way mirrors and sound systems for the preschools and for therapy with children and adults. Diagnostic and treatment techniques taught by our faculty could be observed by a large class seated in an observation room with sound. Our two large light-filled preschool rooms had access to a model playground and between the rooms was a storage room.

However, there were inequities in allocation of space on our two floors which soon began to impinge on the warm spirit that had bound us closely together in our old building. Most of the classroom and clinic life took place on the main floor of our new building, making it busy, crowded, and sometimes noisy. The majority of our graduate students were enrolled in the speech pathology program. All of our clinical services were supervised by specialists in the fields of speech pathology and audiology. But space on the main floor for work was crowded.

Our second floor accommodated our audiology laboratory, a room for use with our new video camera, a library yet to be developed, one secretary, and a few faculty offices. It was quieter and less frequented than the first floor. A very large empty room on the south end of the second floor, the size of both preschool classrooms plus our storage room combined, was reserved for what was intended to be a thriving speech science laboratory. That space was empty when we first moved in, and was still mostly so when I retired in 1982. Probably money to develop the laboratory was not available, as the university was beginning to experience a financial crunch.

I was disappointed at some structural omissions in the preschools as described earlier, but I was determined to be optimistic about the many wonderful new features. We all understood that architectural plans sometimes must be altered to conserve costs, and that it would be expensive to outfit a speech science laboratory.

October 1972: *I made myself very unpopular last week with a mother who was smoking in our crowded waiting room with her new baby close beside her. She was displeased at my suggestion that she extinguish her cigarette. In time our secretaries made brave signs to ban smoking. This was before the time when smoking was prohibited in most public buildings.*

November 1972: *I was walking down the hall in the late afternoon on my way to the janitor's closet to dump my bucket of used water, and saw a large iguana waddling toward me. One clinician along the corridor was calmly corralling her child into a speech therapy cubicle. Other children and clinicians were reacting with startled cries and comments. It was an unusual event in our "three-thirty therapy shuffle." The iguana belongs to the grandmother of one of the hearing impaired children who regularly sits in our waiting room after bringing several children for therapy. Today, to relieve the monotony of the usual trip, she brought her iguana perched on her shoulder sans cage. The iguana had his own ideas of how to proceed once here.*

February 1973: *I am disheartened today. Dan has accepted a position at the University of Arizona and will be leaving us for better opportunities. We will miss his leadership sorely. I can't help but wonder if he is leaving in part because the space in the new building for his program is so out of proportion to its significance. I'm sure that at the University of Arizona he will have a better salary plus strong professional support. I came home tired this evening. Really too tired to write this letter but knowing that after I do, my mind will clear a bit and the day will arrange itself in some perspective. It is only the end of the usual preschool day, eight kids in the morning and eight in the afternoon. But the afternoon was difficult. Mostly little boys who haven't learned to talk the way other kids their age do, and who instead wiggle, make siren or bird noises, run, squirt water at each other at the water table, and generally enhance the life of their teacher, me. Summer is looking good.*

The loss of both Antje and Dan meant fewer faculty members who understood and strongly supported the concept of early childhood education implemented in my classroom. Newly hired staff had other priorities, and it wasn't until Christie joined us in the mid-1970s, to supervise and teach aural rehabilitation, that we had another strong advocate for our kind of early childhood education. In addition to understanding and supporting experiential learning, Christie used a variety of approaches in educating deaf children, including teaching sign language. When our program was closed in 1985, she moved to the University of Colorado, where she soon became a star in her field, chair of her department, then a Dean, and presently receives international recognition as a consultant to aural rehabilitation programs for infants and toddlers around the world.

Women on campus

The 1970s saw the rise of the women's movement and increased consciousness of the status of women on our campus. In our department the women began to compare notes. Our salaries were low and advancement uncertain. Some of our finest teachers were advised that a salary increase depended on publishing research. Some of us who had published were told that our teaching loads, or clinical responsibilities, were not sufficient for promotion. I spoke with our chairman pointing out that if anything should happen to my adventurous traveling husband, I could not support myself and three growing children on my salary. His response was "Well, you'd just have to get another job."

Sensing restlessness without understanding the cause, our director made token decisions at equalizing responsibilities but not salaries. For example, I was appointed advisor to all our freshmen students, and the chief of speech science became advisor to sophomores. This meant another chore for me, although I really liked helping our youngest college students set academic goals. I hope that I didn't lead some of them astray as I encouraged them to explore a variety of interests. I subscribed, then and now, to Joseph Campbell's admonition to "Follow your bliss."

Shortly, the women in our department rebelled and wrote a letter to the Dean. We were invited to talk with him and did so, split into two small groups meeting with him on different days. Shortly after that our director was asked to step-down as chairman, and our chief of audiology, Bob, took his place. Later, when Bob accepted a position in the Pacific Northwest, Karol, always a strong supporter of our early childhood program, became our chairperson. We were delighted with her appointment as it reflected gains for women in status, promotion, and tenure across campus.

In the preschool as well, we began to plan for change.

Transition to mainstreaming

May 1975: *I'm thinking about mainstreaming a few of our younger kids in the morning preschool with children whose language is developing normally. I think that might be a good way to enrich our student training program. Anyhoo, it's the big new trend in special education in Colorado. Recruitment for normally developing kids for our preschool should be easy as several faculty members and graduate students have children the right age and would love to have them "in house." But first, I need to consider the pros and cons.*

Placing "special" children with peers who are not "at risk" in their development was a new idea in public school education for exceptional children, and raised important questions about "acceptance." How will parents react to this change? Will the "special" children be accepted by their playmates? Regarding the attitudes of children, I was convinced it would work well, and it did.

We increased our morning preschool class from eight children to ten to optimize interactions. We included in the new group two or three of our special children who would receive individual speech therapy. The children with normal language did indeed provide models, and, of course, broadened exposure to typical child development for our college students.

There was an explosion of dramatic play indoors and outdoors as the children acted out widely varied new scenarios. Some days we converted the playhouse corner to a beauty parlor with girls sitting under "dryers" while "reading" magazines. The dryers were large ice cream cartons fastened to yardsticks attached to the playhouse chairs. On the playground, children could choose to don fireman hats, noisily climb ladders, and wave hoses to put out fires, or to be sailors on a ship. We reinforced with props whatever interested them at the moment. Mainstreaming was a great success, as it included the development of myriad new topics for play that encouraged imagination and language. Field trips to fire stations and other destinations further enlarged the children's ideas.

At my suggestion, Karol, now chairman of our department, hired a new preschool teacher, Elaine, who provided welcome energy for continuing development of what I now called a "discovery curriculum." Elaine taught the hearing-impaired children in the adjoining preschool classroom. We combined groups for outdoor activities. She had operated a preschool in Boulder, Colorado, and then assisted Winona Graham in developing the training program for preschool teachers, and its playground, at Metropolitan State College in Denver.

Mainstreaming in the public schools eventually created problems. We could select and limit the size of our preschool population, whereas diminishing funds for public school education led to increasing class size and often placed multiply-handicapped children where teachers were overwhelmed. Many conscientious master teachers struggled to do well by each child, but too much was asked of them.

Chapter Six
Continuing to Evolve

Scientists, carpenters, engineers, gardeners, and firefighters at work

I began to keep notes of the things said by the children as they played together. Too often, we teachers focus on what we want to say to children, less often listening carefully to what they tell us. Part of training college students to work with young children is to help them learn to listen closely to what children say, to ask questions of them only to promote further discovery on the part of the child, and to continually observe carefully what children do and how they relate to each other.

Listening to children who talk while they play

May 1976: *I am starting to carry in my pocket a small spiral notebook and am capturing some of the things children say to me and to each other. We were out on the playground today when we heard a siren nearby. Tom, who is always convinced that the world is out to punish the wicked said "It's a policeman." Kurt, who is sure the worst has happened said, "It's a fireman and someone's dead." Buddy, whose mother was arrested last year for possession of narcotics, said "Maybe someone's smoking grass."*

Andy rolled a ball down the slide for Steve to catch. Then did the same with a bucket of water. Ellen and Margie were watching the boys play and started a loud teasing chant to draw attention to themselves, "Yeah, yeah, yeah, you can't catch me." The boys stopped their own game to chase the girls, who then complained to me. I asked the girls if they knew they were interrupting a game the boys were playing? Ellen, hands on hips, responded, "Of course, cuz Steve is my boyfriend." Romance among four-year olds.

Indoors, Mary poured a box of small toys on Margie's head, and admonished her victim, "I'm frustrated, you're supposed to be my friend and you're playing with everybody else."

The children also talked with each other about their art work. Margie painted a large picture with pastel colors, looked at her picture, and told Ellen, "It's summertime when the birds sing. And it's windy. And you can go to the pool." The colors she used were pink, blue, green and yellow. Ellen was completing her painting on the other side of the easel, also using pastel colors, and said, "This is a mountain. That's a flower. A teensy bird. It's summertime."

The artwork of young children reflects developmental maturation just as does every other aspect of their play. First they manipulate paint, then they explore with line and mixing colors. With the development of language, comes representational art—all those wonderful pictures you see posted on elementary school walls of houses, flowers, trees and people.

Socio-dramatic play also follows developmental patterns. As mentioned earlier in the cameo about Tim, imaginative play begins with imitation and develops as children add make-believe in regard to objects, then make-believe in regard to action and situation, followed by persistence in developing a theme, then interacting in make-believe with another child, and finally adding verbal communication. By including normally developing children in our group, our college students had a chance to make new important observations about differences in language at play, and the at-risk children had a chance to have peer models.

With children who talk readily, a teacher has only to pose an occasional casual question to encourage the child's opportunity for discovery. Science materials and unit blocks (which enhance mathematical and engineering concepts) provide many such opportunities. Language-rich play happens when children three to five years old are allowed to choose what interests them, make discoveries, and are free to share their experiences in play together. The foundation for abstract thinking is laid.

Working with children who do not easily engage in group conversation requires thinking of new ways to communicate through action or adult narration as they develop the ability to plan or extend a chosen activity. Something as simple as a teacher, on the floor beside a child at play, moving a toy gas pump next to a "car wash" can lead to expanding a "story." Or sitting beside children at the water table, and putting a ping pong ball and golf ball in the water, can suggest questions about flotation.

When I worked with kindergarten children, I set up the centers for the day's activities before the class assembled. When they arrived, we gathered in an informal circle to talk about what each child wanted to do and set plans for the morning. Options could include play in the playhouse, organizing toys for use in any part of the room, painting at the easel, building with unit blocks, or experimenting with materials set out at a table. If more than two children wanted to paint at our two-sided easel, we discussed "turns" and how they would be arranged.

With children limited in conversational skills, we couldn't make plans as a group at the beginning of each session. Instead, varied play opportunities were set-up to invite children to choose an activity. When they first came to school, choices might be pointed out to them. They soon learned to move quickly to a favorite spot or to join a special friend. With our mainstreamed group we continued this practice.

Those who are new to working with language-impaired children tend to an either-or approach—either you withdraw and do nothing, or you control and the day is teacher directed. One has to develop the art of timing with action to nurture discovery. Science materials provide a unique opportunity in this regard.

Science

Early in the 1960s, Frances Hawkins, a distinguished early childhood educator, was invited to introduce science materials to a class of six deaf preschool children in a Denver public school. Frances had been a teacher of young children and trainer of teachers in Nigeria, Kenya, Uganda and the United States. Her years of experience included work with children from the ages of three to nine. I learned about her new work with deaf preschool children shortly after she completed thirteen mornings once a week with them. When I met with her, I learned that we shared philosophies about educating young children, and we continued to exchange ideas subsequently.

David and Frances Hawkins were conducting research and training teachers to work with science materials at the Mountain View Center for Environmental Education in Boulder. For her experimental work with deaf preschoolers in Denver, Frances and her assistant filled her car with large and small science materials (including an inflatable plastic wading pool for water play) and drove to Denver to spend the morning with six small children, about whom she kept careful records.

Frances' work with hearing-impaired children was described in her 1974 book, *The Logic of Action*. Joseph Featherstone said in *The New Republic* that it was a "mine of practical information as well as deep insights into children's minds and their learning process." Her message was that "The universal language of action is interwoven with the second language, which is spoken." It confirmed the philosophy that we had implemented in our preschool for more than a decade, despite the criticism of some traditional special-education teachers. The Mountain View Center became a primary resource for early childhood educators wanting to develop science materials for their classrooms.

Frances wrote that the "language of action" was also "the language of choice." "We choose as we act, and we act as we choose . . . With open ended raw materials children can be encouraged and trusted to take a large part in the design of their own learning . . . The visible aspects of action-language are but islands— tips of the deeper structure we call reason."

We were still in our old building when I first met Frances. We added many of the ideas generated by her work to our curriculum. For instance, we bought plastic dental trays with small oval indentations to hold water so that children could use eye droppers to experiment with mixing food colors. Warren made pegboards with "feet" for the children to make patterns using golf tees and colored yarn or colored rubber bands.

We made packets of small plastic rectangles in transparent red, blue, yellow and green for the children to play with. The 3" by 5" rectangles were framed with masking tape to protect from sharp edges, and were placed in individual envelopes that could hang on colored yarn around a child's neck. Children could wander the room with these small magic windows, peeking at things and people. When we moved to our new building, we cut large sheets of clear red, blue, and yellow plastic to make three large magic windows for looking outside, mounted at the children's eye levels so they could see the neighborhood and the Rocky Mountains through the colors.

When Elaine joined us, we developed extensive play at the water table. This was too labor intensive for a single teacher in a room without sink and faucet, but manageable for two teachers working together. We bought plastic tubes of varying lengths and diameters to be filled experimentally with water, marbles, or other items to see what happened. Corks in different sizes were available to try closing the ends of the tubes once filled. We added cups, funnels, and syringes for moving water, and ping pong balls and golf balls to explore flotation. Sometimes we had containers with colored water, and sometimes straws and soap mixture for blowing bubbles. Other times we emptied the water table and filled it with sand for play with spoons, containers, sifters, strainers or as landscape for small dinosaur figures or tiny people. (At the indoor table we were less likely than in our outdoor sandbox to lose small figures.)

We had flashlights with batteries to take apart, aluminum containers with lids to fill with seeds, beans, or small rocks for making noise or to classify things which are like each other. We had a bicycle pump to inflate an inner tube or for pretend car repair (tricycles) outdoors.

Our science curriculum was planned to help children discover and explore concepts of liquids, solids, volume, space, air, weight, force, time, sequence, order, patterns and such as we encouraged opportunities for small scientists to learn about their world.

Woodworking and a new playhouse

Woodworking became possible as an outdoor activity. Elaine was experienced in selecting tools and teaching young children how to use them. She built a rabbit hutch for a resident bunny the children could feed, help care for, and invite indoors for special occasions. She planned and developed an addition to our playground deck–a large playhouse with a door and two windows. One window was octagonal and just the right size for climbing in and out. The flat roof of the playhouse became a boat, a train, or whatever was wanted. It had safety fences on three sides with a moveable ladder for firemen or sailors to climb on the open side. Sometimes it was a boat deck for fishermen holding poles to catch fish, or a place to anchor a pulley and rope to experiment with lifting a filled bucket, and sometimes a place for a group to sit together to read a story. The structure had shelves for storing woodworking tools behind doors that could be closed and secured. The outdoor playground became a crowning achievement in my years at the University of Denver.

Sensing a time for me to change

It had been my practice to work only the three academic quarters each year, and to spend summers traveling with my family. Each year I recruited a teacher to replace me for the summer—one who shared my philosophy of education and whom I knew well. By the late 1970s, just before Elaine joined us, I found myself returning in the fall to a playground that needed help. I thought this probably reflected lack of funding for maintenance or lack of interest at higher levels on campus. There certainly was still strong support on the part of our staff, and when Elaine joined us we gained expert help for further development.

My three children were grown and living their own adult lives. One son and his family lived in New Hampshire where he was a university professor. My other son was finishing his doctoral degree in economics at Berkeley and would soon also be a professor. My eighty-two-year old mother lived alone in her own home in southern California.

My husband was at the peak of his career as an international leader in geologic research and had many invitations to lecture and travel. He was invited to be a visiting professor at Yale University in the fall of 1980, and at the University of Amsterdam in the winter of 1981. I wanted to go too, and I wanted to be free to visit my growing family wherever they chose to make their homes. Maybe it was time for me to make a permanent change. A sabbatical would give me a chance to see how that would feel. I asked for and was granted a year's sabbatical.

1980-1981 Off on a lark

The sabbatical year was a great success. I relished being with Warren in New Haven where we set up house sequentially in two different apartments owned by Yale University. I spent my days exploring the campus and environs. On weekends we visited family in New Hampshire, and enjoyed the historic towns of New England. On November 11, I was able to be with my New Hampshire family for the arrival of our first grandson, Dave, whom I christened in my heart our "peace" baby, and to spend time with his sister, Sarah, then three years old.

In Amsterdam, our apartment in a two-hundred year old building overlooked the Herrengracht Canal, and was a block away from the Anne Frank house and museum on the Prinsengracht Canal. I had a vase filled with tulips on our coffee table at all times, and was a Dutch lady waving from my window to the tourist boats passing below. I watched Warren walk each morning over our canal bridge to his large office at the University. I bought fresh fruits and vegetables daily at the tiny store around the corner. From the nearby Damm (central square), I could catch street cars to tour the city. Days I haunted the beautiful museums, and on weekends together we visited countryside and towns by train.

Later, I spent time with my mother in the charming Japanese-style house built for her on a corner lot in Sierra Madre, southern California, right at the foot of the San Gabriel

Mountains. She lived in that house for the rest of her life. I was born in California, and have strong roots there.

Back to the preschool 1981-1982

I was happy to return for the year to our preschool, eager to see how matters were evolving, but also was keenly aware that my own horizons were changing as I explored a new life for myself and thought about setting new goals. The preschool had run smoothly with Elaine and Joanne (psychologist, who had directed the preschools at the University of Colorado Medical Center, and my replacement for the year). Both were experts at nurturing children in what I call Their Magic Years (the title of a book by Selma Fraiberg). We now had a resident bunny, the outdoor playhouse built under Elaine's direction, and a thriving program with mainstreamed preschool children.

One challenge was to plan a presentation for the annual NAEYC meeting in November 1982 in Washington, D.C. I submitted an outline, it was accepted, and I began to develop ideas and photographs for discussion about "Sharing Early Childhood Concepts: An Inter-Disciplinary Model." Four of us from our clinic (Christie, Elaine, Susan, and I) had presented well-received workshops at NAEYC in Atlanta, Georgia in1979, and in San Francisco in 1980. Susan, who has not been introduced earlier in this narrative, was then clinical supervisor of our speech-pathology students. Our workshops were descriptive and anecdotal, illustrated with color slides of preschool children and activities, and were not summaries of research with graphs. The four of us would focus on our training program, our preschool curriculum, and invite questions. The emphasis would be on early childhood education as an opportunity to involve a variety of academic disciplines. However, unexpected surgery to repair my injured knee forced cancellation of the workshop.

Elaine had told me in 1981 that she would not be able to teach after the summer quarter of 1982. Her long commute from Boulder consumed time she needed to be close to her husband, who had a new health challenge. I would miss her energy and support. We took a wonderful field trip with our children to the Museum of Nature and Science, returning to the classroom to construct our own diorama on the floor with small dinosaurs. Clinic staff were awed by the spectacle.

By February of 1982, I knew that it was time for me too to make a change. I wanted to be free to travel with my husband, see more of our scattered family, and take on new projects that included writing about my experiences with teaching young children. I submitted my letter of resignation to the Dean of our college, copy to our chairwoman, in March. It was a very difficult letter to write. My hands shook so badly as I addressed the envelope to the Dean that I had to destroy two envelopes before I got the third one right.

Who would I be if I were not an early childhood educator on the faculty at the University of Denver? Such questions of identity resolve themselves if the change is made at the right time. By electing early retirement, I was ready to walk out one door and live a new life which I had sampled during a sabbatical year. A busy new world opened for me, and continues to unfold with many satisfactions three decades later.

The Department hosted a beautiful retirement party for me at the Phipps Mansion, with cakes baked by faculty members, and champagne. A friend ordered a white orchid corsage for me, which I hesitated to pin on my fragile new chiffon blouse. My mother flew from California to attend, and Warren took many pictures. Following Karol's words of appreciation to me and her comment that they all wondered what I planned to do next, I made a few halting remarks saying that my mother had taught me that "work was love made visible," an acknowledgment of how much I had loved the work I had done. I couldn't read the card signed by our faculty and staff accompanying gifts of a leather travel diary and a shocking pink travel bag because I didn't have my reading glasses with me. I used the travel bag for twenty years, until it wore out.

Before I left our program, I wanted to help secure a teacher to replace me, and to carry the program on to new heights. I suggested Sue, a colleague of mine who had directed the laboratory preschool at Cornell University for several years and was living in Boulder, where her husband was a University of Colorado administrator. I hoped that she would accept Karol's invitation, and she did. Sue created at D.U. what she called a "storybook curriculum," and prepared to write about it. Two other teachers were hired to help her, and she became free to implement a true laboratory experience for our college students helping in the preschool with regular times for supervisory feedback.

Irreversible change 1985

Sadly, the preschool continued for only three more years. In 1985, our department and its clinical program were abolished in a campus-wide effort to make programs cost-effective. Our clinical services and graduate studies were expensive to operate. Both had been part of the University since the 1940s. The classroom in our new building was dedicated by an alumna to an early director, Ruth Clark, a colorful pioneer and beloved faculty member in speech pathology, in the 1950s and early 1960s. Ruth's students recalled fondly how they had speculated before her lectures about which handbag and matching shoes she would wear that day. After much angst and protest on the part of alumni, faculty, students and clients, the department was terminated in 1985. Our building became space for other offices, and my beloved designer playground was scraped, leaving only a grassy hill and a picnic table. I believe that today that corner of the campus is near the parking garage for the handsome Newman Center for the Performing Arts.

Afterwords

My story afterward is in several parts. I did travel overseas extensively with my husband, and also visited members of my family frequently. On visits to New England, I became fascinated by the story of my mother's family, most of whom had come to New England in the 17th century. Mother was unaware of their early stories until I began on-site family research. I discovered that I loved to do historical research and used travel opportunities to pursue on-site research in this country and abroad.

I rejoined the League of Women Voters, of which I had been a member before DU days. As a member of the board of directors of the LWV of Jefferson County for six years, I held the portfolio for social policy. In this role, I used my training as a sociologist to conduct research regarding health care, education, welfare policies, and housing in my County. I affirmed my new identity with business cards indicating that I was an "early childhood specialist."

In the first decade of the new century, my enthusiasm turned to helping establish a continuing education program for adults fifty years and older on the west side of metropolitan Denver. OLLI West was begun as an extension of a program funded by the Osher Lifelong Learning Institute with a grant to the University of Denver. The program operates from universities across the country. As I made the transition from years of interest in education for the very young, I have come to the place where I am right now— full circle in the mandala of my life.

Chapter Seven
Reflections

My intent in writing this memoir is to describe my experiences over twenty years as an early childhood educator, fulfilling a promise made to myself and to several mentors after I left the university in 1982. I am glad now that I delayed writing that account. It would have been a text for preschool teachers working with special young children–to be added to a plethora of books now gathering dust on shelves. It would have had chapters on child development, curriculum, how to train college students, work with parents, observe children, and write summary reports. It would have included an extensive bibliography and referenced footnotes.

Instead I have written a personal memoir, which I hope will be of value to others interested in early childhood education as well as to my family and friends. It is an account of what I did and why. It tells what I believe about preschool education. It is a narrative of my own development, and of how much I learned from children, parents, college students, and my colleagues.

My belief in the importance of play as the primary means of providing education for young children is paramount. Play is the work of the young child, and guided play with other children provides the foundation for symbolic thought in later years. Woven throughout this memoir are two other stories. One is the interface of my professional life with my personal world, and the other is the impact of social change generated by the civil rights and women's movements of the 1960s-1970s. Those two motifs may resonate with other women, other lives.

I was a working mother of three children, a woman faculty member on a university campus, a teacher of young children, and a citizen of the larger community of early childhood educators. I was married to a globe-trotting husband who spent months in the Antarctic studying the geology of that continent, and later worked in Southeast Asia and elsewhere. His social milieu and accomplishments created a very different world for me at home as partner and hostess, with a sometimes frustrating disconnect from my work role. These intersecting threads comprise the drama and message of this memoir.

We find ourselves today at a new crossroad for early childhood education, challenged by major national changes. Universal preschool education has been suggested to mitigate social inequities. Who should fund it? Who should plan it? Who should teach? What should they teach? Who will provide oversight? I urge that we pause long enough to reflect seriously on what is happening to the process of educating our young children and to consider our goals for their future. Our educational institutions have become so large and complex that they often seem unresponsive to individual parents, children, and families.

There is presently increased pressure to stress academic programs earlier in life than we do now. I believe this is counter-productive. We know that it is possible to teach three-year-olds to read, but the question is, why do we want to? David Elkind (Tufts University) discussed the issue of pushing children ahead prematurely in his book, *The Hurried Child*. The preschool is the upward extension of the home and the extension downward of the public school. Let's start at this intersection of our two primary socializing institutions, the family and the school, and see what we can do to promote optimal development for our youngest children. The demands of increasingly sophisticated technology require that special attention be directed toward developing creative critical thinkers. The foundation for symbolic and abstract thinking is laid in the play of young children interacting with each other as they explore their world. Play must be part of how children are cared for today, yet that faces fierce challenges.

And what about the special young child at risk for developing language? The issue of compensatory training versus experiential learning has been discussed over the years. One response lies in the belief that all children are special, each is unique, and children are more like each other than different in basic sequential development. A child crawls before he stands, stands before he walks, walks before he hops, hops before he skips. My goal would be to give all children time to play with other children in enriched indoor and outdoor environments, with teachers as planners and helpers. When individual help for disabilities is needed, my hope is that it can be provided in addition to, not instead of, play in a preschool.

As parenting has changed, so have the options for child care, many of which exclude opportunities for the kind of play experiences described in this book. Historically, care of young children was the responsibility of a mother (or mother substitute), which often led to a young mother feeling isolated. But some mothers, then and now, enjoy sharing substantial time with their babies and preschoolers, and are able to choose to do so. Many other women choose to have professional careers, while at the same time the number of families where both mothers and fathers must work to support households has grown. T. Berry Brazelton (Harvard) campaigned on behalf of legislation supporting the Family and Medical Leave Act for mothers wanting leave time to bond with their new infants. He believed strongly that there should be time for working mothers to be at home with their babies. In addition there are many single parent families. All want the best possible care for their children. Obviously, no single plan can fit all needs.

We now find ourselves with a smorgasbord of care-giving options. We have public and private preschool programs, Head Start Centers, and licensed and unlicensed day-care workers caring for children in private homes. The large for-profit franchised day-care center, operated at low cost to be affordable for young families, was highlighted in a journal article years ago titled "Kentucky Fried Children, The Child Care Problem," by Joseph Featherstone, who lamented warehousing of small children. A significant problem in these centers is frequent turnover of personnel because of low pay, which makes it hard for small children to build relationships with caring adults. Educators Burton White (Harvard) and James Hymes (University of Maryland) argue rightly that close relationships are critical for optimal development of young children.

We also have programs that offer preschool classes in French, ballet, reading, and computer skills. In some preschools curriculum materials are kept in drawers or on shelves with labels indicating that the contents facilitate "personal-social" or "intellectual" development, or "fine motor coordination." Some private preschools offer packaged programs guaranteed to provide "reading readiness" before kindergarten. Some waiting lists for elite preschools in large cities imply that it is wise to enroll infants "early" in order to qualify for a place in a long line of "right" schools leading to the Ivy League. On the other hand, I remember being told in 1954 by other mothers in my new suburban Colorado neighborhood that the most important requirement for my kindergarten-bound son was to be able to tie his shoelaces.

In making plans, the question is asked "What does the preschool teach?" The answer should be science, music, art, literature, math, all of the subjects in a college catalog—but at levels appropriate for young children. This means nurturing a love of books and stories, experimenting with materials, and playing imaginatively and vigorously indoors and outdoors with other children their age.

Along the way we have lost regard for teachers of young children. Witness the low salaries paid to day care and kindergarten personnel, the drop in federal and state funded preschool programs across the nation, and the emotional media discussions about mothers who stay at home and those who "work." Teacher training reflects these changes in attitude, and is of necessity focused on what a child care worker needs to know in order to meet licensing requirements rather than on the quality of education. There are courses to train Nannies.

We must be concerned with meeting the developmental needs of young children: to form an ongoing relationship with a caring adult; to be treated with consistency and unconditional love; to be seen as a child, not a miniature adult. Children's needs seem to have become secondary to cost, convenience, malpractice suits, personal ambition and fulfillment, all fueled by pressure on children to get ready for first grade, high school, and the "best" college.

Powerful evidence that the most important financial investments we can make are in the first five years of life, and that these investments more than pay for themselves, is documented by James Heckman, Nobel Prize economist at the University of Chicago, and his associates. (See the reading-list monograph by Cunha, Heckman, Lochman, and Masterov.) Doing less puts the future of our society at risk.

Our basic questions should be, what do we want for our children? What kind of people are we hoping to nurture? Understanding and accepting that they are not simply extensions of ourselves, knowing, as Khalil Gibran wrote, "We cannot give them our thoughts, only our love . . . they come through us not from us . . . an expression of life's longing for itself."

Asking these questions will lead us to consider global issues: the quality of the physical world in which these children will live, and the air, water, earth we leave as our legacy to them; the capacity for cooperation among the humans sharing Planet Earth.

We know we must enhance each child's sense of herself as an individual, and her feelings of self-worth and competence. The adults in a child's life are the mirror in which she sees a looking-glass self. What does that say about the role of the adult in the earliest years of childhood? James Hymes suggested in his book, *A Child Development Point of View*, that the first preschool teacher should be a "honey" to the child, offering a loving, caring relationship that builds trust and frees the child to optimize learning.

If you are planning for a year, sow rice.
If you are planning for a decade, plant trees.
If you are planning for a lifetime, educate a child.

Chinese proverb

Suggested Reading

Brazelton, T. Berry. *Working and Caring*. New York: Addison Wesley, 1983.

Cunha, Flavio, James J. Heckman, Lance Lochner, and Dmitry V. Masterov. *Interpreting the evidence on life cycle skill formation*. Cambridge, MA: National Bureau of Economic Research, Working Paper 11331, 168 pp., 2005; available without charge at www.nber.org/papers/w11331.pdf. (Also published in Handbook of the Economics of Education, Elsevier, 2006.)

Elkind, David. *The Power of Play, Learning What Comes Naturally*. Boston: Da Capo Press, 2007.

Elkind, David. *The Hurried Child*. Boston: DaCapo Press, 2008.

Featherstone, Joseph. "Kentucky Fried Children. The Day Care Problem," The New Republic, v. 163, October 11, 1970, p. 12-16.

Gibran, Khalil. *The Prophet*. New York: Alfred A. Knopf, Sixty-second printing, 1960.

Graham, Winona. *First Encounters. A History of Early Childhood Education in Colorado*. Privately published adaptation of PhD thesis, University of Denver, 1983.

Hamilton, Alicita. "A Preschool Program for Children with Limited Hearing," Young Children, v. 21, p. 267-271, 1966.

Hart, Betty, and Todd R. Risley. *Meaningful Differences in the Everyday Experience of Young American Children*. Baltimore: Brookes Publishing, 1995.

Hawkins, Frances P. *The Logic of Action. Young Children at Work*. New York: Pantheon House, 1974.

Hymes, James L. *Teaching the Child Under Six*. Columbus Ohio: Chas. E. Merrill, 1968.

Hymes, James L. *A Child Development Point of View*. New York: Prentice-Hall, 1955.

Piaget, Jean. *The Language and Thought of the Child*. New York: New American Library, 1974.

Read, Katherine H. *The Nursery School: A Human Relationships Laboratory*. Philadelphia: W. B. Saunders, 1968.

Rosenberg, Tina. "The Power of Talking to Your Baby," New York Times, April 10, 2013.

Spencer, Kyle. "With Blocks, Educators Go Back to Basics," New York Times, November 27, 2011.

White, Burton L. *The First Three Years of Life*. New York: Fireside Books, 1995.

About the Author

Alicita Hamilton was a member of the faculty and staff of the University of Denver Speech and Hearing Clinic, and the Department of Speech Pathology and Audiology, from 1962 to 1982. She directed preschool classes with changing populations, first of hearing-impaired children, then of children with diverse communication disorders, and finally normally-developing and at-risk children together. She trained college students in clinical programs how to work with small children, taught academic courses in parent counseling and in interviewing, lectured on child development in various other classes, and participated in several research projects.

Alicita received a B.A. in child psychology from Scripps College, Claremont, California, in 1948, where she first worked with educating young children, and an M.A. in sociology of the family from the University of Denver in 1968. She taught kindergarten in a public school in Inglewood, California, and, during 1960-1962, preschool in Lakewood, Colorado. She presented local and national workshops describing her work. She served as a president of the Colorado Association for the Education of Young Children, established that organization's first scholarship for a student of early childhood education, and funded the scholarship initially with proceeds from the book she edited, *Colorado Gold*.